D1243696

Black Feminism
in Contemporary Drama

Lisa M. Anderson

University of Illinois Press
Urbana and Chicago

Library of Congress Cataloging-in-Publication Data
Anderson, Lisa M., 1966–
Black feminism in contemporary drama /
Lisa M. Anderson.
p.   cm.
Includes bibliographical references and index.
ISBN=13 978-0-252-03228-8 (cloth : acid-free paper)
ISBN=10 0-252-03228-4 (cloth : acid-free paper)
1. American drama—African American authors—History
and criticism. 2. Feminist drama—History and criticism.
3. American drama—Women authors—History and
criticism. 4. Feminism and literature—United States.
5. African Americans in literature.
I. Title.
PS338.N4A48   2008
812'.609896073—dc22   2007015804

Contents

Acknowledgments   vii

1. A Black Feminist Theatre Emerges   1

2. Pearl Cleage's Black Feminism   17

3. We Are the Daughters of Aunt Jemima: Remembering
   Black Women's History   35

4. Battling Images: Suzan-Lori Parks and Black Iconicity   55

5. Kia Corthron's Everyday Black Women   76

6. Signifying Black Lesbians: Dramatic Speculations   95

7. A Black Feminist Aesthetic   115

Notes   127

Bibliography   133

Index   141

Acknowledgments

There are many people without whom this book would never have been written. It was not the book I was planning to write, and I began writing two other books before I realized that this book was emerging from other work that I was doing. In a discussion, my colleague, Neal Lester helped me realize that I was writing essays that might work together as a book.

I am greatly indebted to my colleagues in the Women and Gender Studies Program at Arizona State University, whose support and encouragement helped me to realize this book in its physical state. Particularly, I would like to thank Karen Leong and Ann Hibner Koblitz, who read drafts of the manuscript and offered excellent suggestions for editing. The Women's Studies Reading Group was also vitally important in providing suggestions that improved the manuscript's focus, and suggested other ways that I might elaborate and expand the proto-book. I am also grateful to Mary Rothschild and Mary Margaret Fonow, both of whom were my program chairs during the time that I worked to complete this manuscript, and to Rose Weitz, who helped me to keep my writing on track when there were entirely too many distractions. My colleagues in the School of Theatre and Film, especially Margaret Knapp, Stephani Etheridge Woodson, Tamara Underiner, and Ramon Rivera-Servera have also provided intellectual support and guidance.

I have also had the great fortune to work with a superb editor, Joan Catapano, and her indefatigable editors and assistants. Few things can compare to working with a great editor, and I very much appreciate their work and support on this book. Joan also chose reviewers who provided me with excellent feedback, and I thank them as well. This project was partially supported by a Women's Studies Summer Research Grant, and an earlier College of Liberal Arts and Sciences Faculty Grant-in-Aid supported research that indirectly helped with the writing of this book.

Sharon Bridgforth provided me not only with manuscripts of her work, but a sustained conversation about her work. I am humbled by her talent, and encouraged by her visions. I am glad that I am able, in this work, to expose more people to her incredible work. The three-way conversation that emerged between myself, Sharon, and Joni Jones at the Association for Theatre in Higher Education conference in 2002 allowed me to gain a deeper understanding of Sharon's work. In addition to Joni, I would like to thank Jennifer Devere Brody, David Krasner, and Stephanie Batiste for their support of my work.

I could not do any of my work without the support, advice, and love of my partner and my family. Jackie Martínez keeps me sane, happy, and challenges me to think in more complex ways. During the long, long process of my working on this book, she has done everything from reading chapter drafts to walking the dogs when I needed to write. *Gracias, querida.*

To my ancestors, and those who came before me—theorists and artists (who are so often one in the same).

1 A Black Feminist Theatre Emerges

Looking back on the twentieth century, most scholars consider Ntozake Shange's *for colored girls who have considered suicide/when the rainbow is enuf* as the piece that heralded the arrival of something we might call "black feminist theatre." Although feminist theatre scholars have written critical works on plays by black women playwrights, the clear, cogent concept of a black feminist theatre remains elusive. That is not to say that there is not, or has not been, black feminist theatre; it means only that black feminist writing about black feminist theatre has been scarce. As a testament to that scarcity, while Errol Hill and James Hatch list much of the contemporary scholarship on African American theatre at the end of their extraordinary *A History of African American Theatre,* there is no section on black feminist theatre or black feminist writing about theatre. In fact, in the index of this seminal work, there are only three references to feminist theatre or feminism.

Black feminist theatre does in fact exist. It consists of playwrights, directors, performance artists, and scholars who, intentionally or not, blend the core values and aesthetics of black feminism with their art and scholarship. Like black feminism itself, the origins of a theatre that we might call both black and feminist extend back to the end of the nineteenth century and the beginning of the twentieth. Like black feminism itself, black feminist theatre has changed and grown, particularly in the last quarter of the twentieth century and the beginning of the twenty-first. This project attempts to frame, or construct, a contemporary black feminist theatre aesthetic by looking to the works themselves, in the spirit of Barbara Christian's "The Race for Theory," but also by applying the concepts that have come to define black feminism specifically. The classic works of black feminist scholars—Patricia Hill Collins, Hazel V. Carby, Barbara Christian, Barbara Smith, Valerie Smith, Deborah E. McDowell, bell hooks, and many others—is the ground beneath my feet. Their efforts to mark the terrain of black feminism, black feminist aesthetics, and black feminist literary criticism make this work possible.

The impetus for finding something that I could call a "black feminist aesthetic" emerged out of my research in both black and feminist theory and criticism. By "aesthetics" I mean not some objective "beauty" of the text. I mean here the context in which a work is situated, how its construction and production are shaped, and how that shaping is informed by its politics. The question of the function of theatre and performance has always been a central one in drama created by and for black Americans, from the early efforts of the African Grove Company to contemporary playwrights and theatre companies. In the early part of the twentieth century, particularly in the period of the Harlem Renaissance, the function of art was contested (particularly as evidenced by the Du Bois–Locke debate), but production and reception of theatre remained open.[1] In other words, the existence of competing opinions about the function of art enabled the creation of dramas that depicted a range of black existence. Drama (indeed, literature) of the Harlem Renaissance included many different kinds of blacks. Plays such as Willis Richardson's *The Chip Woman's Fortune,* Georgia Douglas Johnson's *A Sunday Morning in the South,* and Langston Hughes's *Mulatto* depicted the lives of poor blacks in the rural South. The struggles of working-class blacks of the urban North were captured by plays like Angelina Weld Grimké's *Rachel* and Alice Dunbar Nelson's *Mine Eyes Have Seen.* Although the middle-class black experience was not typically the subject of dramatic literature, novelists like Nella Larsen gave readers a glimpse into the lives of middle-class blacks of the urban North. The majority, but not all, of the characters were noble, designed to reveal the humanity and dignity of blacks in the face of racism. There were also the church gossips of Eulalie Spence's *Fool's Errand,* and Emmaline in Zora Neale Hurston's *Color Struck,* and other characters who were not designed or intended to demonstrate the nobility of black lives but the reality of a diverse people. During the 1940s, however, ideas about the function of black literature shifted in such a way that restricted the possibilities of representation. Their struggles against racism were constructed as conflict between black and white men; where women appeared, both black and white women were often obstacles to the achievement of liberation. Richard Wright's novels are often cited as prime examples of the 1940s black aesthetic.

As "the" black aesthetic attempted to remove gender from a codified authentic blackness or black experience, feminist theory and aesthetics imagined a female identity uncomplicated by race or class. Feminist dramatic theory and criticism, while not necessarily attempting to create a monolithic feminist theory, approached theatre and drama from the perspective of the white, middle-class woman, much as the second-wave feminist focused on the experiences of white, middle-class women. Because both of these aesthetics excluded the possibility (and the work) of a black feminist aesthetic, it became necessary for black feminist literary critics to develop a black feminist aesthetic. Now, it is necessary to outline an aesthetic of black feminist drama and performance.

By engaging in this project, I have attempted to begin to fill a gap in feminist theory and criticism of drama and performance. In her essay "The Race for Theory," Barbara Christian argues that rather than invent a theory of how we ought to read, "we need to read the works of our writers in our various ways and remain open to the intricacies of the intersection of language, class, race, and gender in the literature" (337). My uncovering of something that we can call a black feminist aesthetic requires an investigation of the texts themselves; open to what the texts have to offer, I explore the commonalities between and among the works of some contemporary writers with a knowledge of the history and tradition of black women's playwriting and dramatic performance. I hope to uncover what "black feminist drama" has looked like and, more specifically, what it looks like at the beginning of the new century. Because the central focus of this text is on more contemporary works, it does not delve into the foundational works of black feminist dramatists and performers; there is much critical work on playwrights such as Lorraine Hansberry, Alice Childress, Ntozake Shange, and Adrienne Kennedy. The playwrights whose work I discuss in this text are not the only contemporary black feminist playwrights. I have also chosen to concentrate on these artists—Pearl Cleage, Breena Clarke, Glenda Dickerson, Suzan-Lori Parks, Kia Corthron, Shirlene Holmes, and Sharon Bridgforth—not because they are the only contemporary black feminist playwrights, but rather because they allow me to look at a range of writing styles, performance styles, and generational differences.

Other black feminist literary critics have delineated some of this aesthetic. As Madhu Dubey writes, black feminist literary criticism has focused on "discourse on stereotypes versus character" and "affirmation of oral folk culture as the source of a uniquely black feminine literary authority" (2). I have let the words and stories of black women artists reveal the theory and the aesthetic of contemporary black feminism. The central questions of such an aesthetic include whether or not the text critiques, shifts, or alters representations from dominant culture stereotype, and whether or not the text is structurally consistent with the goals of the "community." This aesthetic also considers questions on the function of the art. What has emerged is not monolithic; not surprisingly, what shapes the black *feminisms* of these writers shifts with their identities.

Nineteenth-Century Black Feminist Beginnings

Beverly Guy-Sheftall's anthology *Words of Fire: an Anthology of African-American Feminist Thought,* begins in the nineteenth century with the writings and speeches of women like Anna Julia Cooper, Sojourner Truth, Maria Stewart, Mary Church Terrell, and Ida B. Wells-Barnett. It is here, at the critical point in U.S. history when the rights of women and blacks began to be asserted, that black women first stressed the intersection of race and sex. They understood the complex ways in which discrimination on the basis of race and sex affected their lives, and they worked toward the dual goals of rights for women and blacks. As Cooper wrote, "The colored woman of to-day occupies, one may say, a unique position in this country. . . . She is confronted by both a woman question and a race problem, and is as yet an unknown or an unacknowledged factor in both" (45). Cooper's words demonstrate the early understanding of what contemporary feminism refers to as *intersectionality.*

Cooper's first enunciation of a black feminism was concerned with the civil rights of both women and blacks. That commitment is evident in works by writers and activists like Ida B. Wells-Barnett, whose tireless activism against lynching benefited black women and men. For other writers, women's contributions to African American society were invaluable. The black women of the emergent middle class and "talented tenth" combined their efforts to assist black women of all socioeconomic classes in asserting themselves as *women,* and could separate themselves from the fictions and stereotypes associated with black women in their roles as slave women. As Mary Church Terrell wrote, "To-day in each and every section of the country there are hundreds of homes among colored people, the mental and moral tone of which is as high and as pure as can be found among the best people of any land. To the women of the race may be attributed in large measure the refinement and purity of the colored home" (Terrell 65). Their emphasis was on dissuading white Americans of the alleged moral inferiority of blacks, and especially of black women.

A Renaissance for Women's Issues

The next period in the development of black feminism coincided not only with the early twentieth-century suffragist movement, but also with the Harlem Renaissance. As would be typical, women's writings from this period would be largely lost until the recovery projects of the 1980s, when scholars worked assiduously to recover the writings of women of previous generations. In spite of their temporary loss, the values of black feminism in this era changed little from those of the previous generation. Women like Angelina Weld Grimké, Elsie Johnson McDougald, Alice Dunbar Nelson, and Amy Garvey would continue to agitate on the issues important to black women—oppression based on race *and* gender. Like their intellectual descendants in the 1980s, these women would argue that the liberation of *peoples* of African descent necessitated the liberation of *women* of African descent. Middle-class women activists concerned themselves with voting rights (including the voting rights of black men in the South), gaining access to birth control, and educating black children about black history. All of these issues, and others, would characterize the artistic production of black women during the Renaissance period. As evidenced by Kathy A. Perkins's anthology of black women playwrights before 1950, several plays focused on the importance of access to birth control; some plays were even published in the *Birth Control Review*. Perkins and Judith Stephens edited an anthology of antilynching plays, another issue of great concern for black women. The plays of Perkins's first anthology provide evidence of the importance of social and political issues for women playwrights during the first part of the twentieth century.

A majority of these plays focuses on the experiences of black women, whether dealing with the aftereffects of lynching or the personal problems of colorism. Unlike the nineteenth century, when black theatre was confined to the ignominies of the minstrel show, the early twentieth century provided opportunities in the forms of play contests and emergent university and community theatre in which such plays could be performed. For example, both Mary P. Burrill and Angelina Weld Grimké taught at the M Street School (Dunbar High School in Washington, D.C.), and both were playwrights who taught playwriting to their students. Alain Locke's influence would help encourage students at Howard University, where he founded the Howard Players and wrote influential articles such as "Steps Toward the Negro Theatre." It is during this period, I argue here, that what will come to be known as black or African American feminist theatre begins.

Literature—whether drama, poetry, or fiction—was one of the primary methods for expressing social and political activism for black Americans during the 1920s and 1930s. The popularity of the Harlem Renaissance for black and white readers alike was one element that led to this artistic surge. In addition, the educational advancements argued by the previous generation at the end of the nineteenth century made possible the legions of black teachers who were willing and able to bring this material to their students. The political issues of the day, including the domestic aftermath of World War I and the postwar treatment of black soldiers, and the incorporation of the NAACP and the National Urban League, made activism more accessible to more people.

The issues of black feminists in this period were evident explicitly in the plots of the extant works of Renaissance-period writers. Their engagement in these issues has been the subject of articles and critical works, including my *Mammies No More: The Changing Image of Black Women on Stage and Screen*, Elizabeth Brown-Guillory's *Their Place On The Stage: Black Women Playwrights In America*, and Carol P. Marsh-Lockett's *Black Women Playwrights: Visions on the American Stage*. However, it is worth investigating the specific elements of black feminism in its manifestations in these plays.

Whether of the rural South or the urban North, many of these plays center on the experiences of women. Grimké's 1917 *Rachel* attacks black unemployment and underemployment and colorism, and ultimately questions the validity of bringing black children into a world where their rights are systematically denied. Georgia Douglas Johnson's folk plays also center on women; in her plays, women of the South struggle to maintain family in the face of lynching, miscegenation, and the rape of black women by white men. Her attention to the issues of rape and miscegenation are explored in *Blue Blood,* for example, where the mothers of an engaged couple discover that they were both raped by the same white man, who is the father of both children. The tragedy of their assaults enables the children, both of whom are in love with other people, to break their engagement. The reason for the match was that both children, because of their white father, were valued for their lighter skin; both children actually desired people who were darker than they were. In both *A Sunday Morning in the South* and *Blue-Eyed Black Boy,* a young man is in danger of being lynched; of the two, the blue-eyed boy is saved by his white father, while Tom, who has only his old grandmother to protect him, is murdered. Zora Neale Hurston's *Color Struck* and *Polk County* both deal with the problems faced by black women around the issue of skin color. Her dark-skinned characters are challenged by their hatred of their skin color, even while others around them do not share their bias. Mary Burrill's *They That Sit in Darkness* questions the unavailability of birth control methods and education. The devastating effects of the lack of birth control are felt when the protagonist must abandon her plans for college because her mother dies following the birth of her tenth child, leaving her to care for her siblings.

Though not all of these plays were performed, they were published and read in a variety of sources. And while Alain Locke advocated for art for art's sake, these women made serious statements about the lives of black women and the challenges that faced them in the early twentieth century.

Civil Rights, Women's Rights, and the Birth of Black Feminism

After World War II and the surge in civil rights activity and protest, black women attempted to maintain their multifront struggles. Though the primary faces and personages of the civil rights era were men, black women continued their activism without much large-scale fanfare. Women like Ella Baker energized young men and women, working on the front lines of the civil rights struggle. Other women housed students from the Student Nonviolent Coordinating Committee (SNCC) in their houses so that they could continue their activist work in the South. By this point, black women had a much more prominent role in the theatre in a variety of roles. Lorraine Hansberry had already won the New York Drama Critics Circle Award in 1959 for *A Raisin in the Sun;* Alice Childress and Adrienne Kennedy were writing plays that were being produced in New York and in regional theatres around the country.

These black women playwrights of the late 1950s and early 1960s would herald the dawning of the black feminist scholarship that would emerge in the early 1970s. Though they may not all have claimed the label "feminist," I argue here that, like their foremothers in the Renaissance, the politics and aesthetics of their work were undoubtedly black feminist drama.

Hansberry and Feminism

A Raisin in the Sun (1959) marked a peak in black feminist playwriting. As Sheri Parks asserts, the uncut version of the play places "the play back into the center of black women's concerns for the continuity of the culture and survival of self and family" (200). Though *Raisin* is often considered Walter Lee's play (as the protagonist), the women of the play are central to it. Hansberry was unequivocally a feminist; in fact, she preceded many white mainstream feminists by reading—and fully engaging—Simone de Beauvoir's *The Second Sex* in French in the 1957. Her review was unfinished, but it reveals that Hansberry was not only a gifted intellectual, but that she was acutely aware of the status of women. She writes:

> Today in the United States our national attitude toward women and their place, or finding it, is one of frantic confusion. Women themselves are among the foremost promoters of the confusion. They have been born into a cultural heritage which has instructed them of a role to play without question and in the main they are willing to do so. And yet, therein hangs the problem: housework, "homemaking," are drudgery; it is inescapable, women flee it in one form or another. They do not always understand their own rebellion, or why they want to rebel or why *they* deprecate, more than anyone else really, what the rest of the nation will always insist, so long as it does not have to do

it, is the "cornerstone" of our culture, the "key" to our civilization, and the "bedrock foundation" of our way of life. (137)

In all of Hansberry's works, she engages points of intersectionality. Her feminist perspective suffuses each of her plays, even though they are not singularly focused on gender. For example, women are not the focus of *Les Blancs,* but gender—and racialized gender roles—are important elements of the play. In this play, she examines the complicated power structures and differentials in colonialism, particularly colonialism that is on the verge of being overthrown. The character of the Warrior Woman, the only woman of African descent in the play, is vitally important to the ability of Tshembe and the consciousness that urges him to act. Her unfinished script *The Drinking Gourd,* set during slavery, deals frankly with the problems and concerns of slave life and questions of liberation.

Raisin in the Sun addresses several issues of importance to black feminism. First, Lena Younger emphasizes the importance of the community and community values. Her opposition to Walter Lee's investment in a liquor store is part of her Christian values system; in this, she reflects the issues and concerns of 1990s womanist theorists. Lena believes that owning a liquor store in a struggling community would not contribute to the betterment of that community, but rather detract from its possibility. Beneatha's choice to pursue a career as a doctor and not, as her brother encourages, a nurse, captures the arguments of the mainstream women's movement for the ability of women to pursue careers previously thought of as men's careers. Finally, Ruth must decide whether or not to have what was then an illegal abortion. Ruth's crisis is based upon her family's poverty and the additional resources required to raise another child; in this, Hansberry's argument is similar to those of the early black birth control advocates. Of course, Lena's Christian beliefs discourage such an action, and because of her purchase of a house, Ruth is able to choose to continue her pregnancy.

Hansberry understood that she lived at the intersection of race and gender; as Margaret Wilkerson so eloquently states in the introduction to *Lorraine Hansberry: The Collected Last Plays,* "Her consciousness, of both ethnicity and gender from the very beginning, brought awareness of two key forces of conflict and oppression in the contemporary world" (7). While her other plays may not seem to have focused on gender, her feminism always at least peeked through. It was impossible for it *not* to: "fundamental to this comprehensive world-view, however, was Hansberry's insistence upon a thorough probing of the individual within the specifics of culture, ethnicity and gender" (8).

Hansberry is not the only woman playwright of the 1950s and '60s whose work I characterize as feminist. As Thelma Shinn writes, Hansberry is joined by Adrienne Kennedy, Alice Childress, and Ntozake Shange as "agents of change" (150). She continues, "each of these four writers has offered a unique perspective on their common concerns of the racial and gender limitations on both their human and social definitions of self" (150). The plays of Adrienne Kennedy deal frankly with the intersections of race and gender, with her protagonists agonizing over their mixed heritage and the expectation that they live up to a white ideal of "womanhood." Characters who populate her early plays, like *Funnyhouse of a Negro* and *The Owl Answers,* deal with these two issues that have long faced African American women. Her reformulation of the tragic mulatta icon centers the tragic in the circumstances created for her by living in a predominantly white and racist society. In *The Owl Answers,* her protagonist is the product of a white father and black mother, who is unacknowledged by that white father. This situation, whether the relationship was consensual or not, has a long history in the United States, and has been an issue of concern for black proto-feminists and feminists.

Alice Childress's work addressed other concerns of black women. Her early play *Trouble in Mind* dealt explicitly with the effects of racism on the possibilities open to young blacks interested in pursuing a career in the arts. *The Wedding Band* engages the issue of interracial relationships and the continued struggle against racism. One element of the play is that it emphasizes the *community* of a black community; when the protagonist falls in love with a white man, the community accepts her relationship with him even while his family does not. *Wine in the Wilderness* indicts the black intelligentsia of the 1960s for their inability to see beyond class. It is also a resounding critique of black men's ideas about black womanhood; they worship an "African Queen" who is only imaginary, while black women who have struggled to survive and are consistently overlooked walk among them.

Childress's feminism speaks through Tommy, a.k.a. Tomorrow Marie. Cynthia, the well-meaning black social worker, attempts to explain the evils of the black matriarchal society to Tommy, who grew up in a single-mother household. Tommy responds, "We didn't have nothin' to rule over, not a pot nor a window. And my papa picked hisself up and run off with some finger-poppin' woman and we never hear another word 'til ten, twelve years later when a undertaker call up and ask if Mama wanta come claim his body." (760–61). Tommy understands from life experience that the black matriarchy is a myth, not reality. In her scene with Cynthia, she proves that she has more knowledge and understanding, even though she is not educated, than the educated and assimilated Cynthia. When Cynthia asserts that "you have to let the Black man have his manhood again," Tommy responds, "I didn't take it from him, how I'm gonna give it back?" (761). At every turn, Childress's 1969 play echoes the black feminism that is emerging.

Black Feminist Criticism and *for colored girls*

When *for colored girls who have considered suicide/when the rainbow is enuf* premiered in December 1974, it was like a bolt of lightning. Shange, who drew some of her inspiration from the women's studies program at Sonoma State College, created a collaborative poem—a "choreopoem"—that examined and expressed the varied lives and tribulations of black women in the United States. Because of the traditions on which Shange drew, this piece of theatre could not help but be feminist. Critical responses by black men were largely negative. Like Alice Walker's *The Color Purple* would be in 1982, *for colored girls* was lambasted for being anti-male, particularly anti–black male. Probably the most insistent was Robert Staples, but he was joined by numerous other black men and women who protested Shange's alleged misrepresentation of black men. *for colored girls* was the second play by a black woman produced on Broadway; it won Obie, Tony, Grammy, and Audelco awards, among others. As Neal Lester explains, however, "rather than consider Shange's whole picture of male-female relationships, these critics try to deny or justify the males' abusive behaviors in the choreopoem" (319).

for colored girls remains one of the most influential plays by black women playwrights. Shange's choreopoem captured the lives of black women as they moved from childhood into adulthood, from segregation to integration, from joy to pain and back to joy. As Shange said, "black women, to be represented at all, must themselves do the writing" (Burke 184). When we first encounter the Ladies, they are all "outside" cities; they experience marginalization through their experiences at the intersections of multiple oppressions. They move from this place to one of self-love and self-acceptance, which is the most important move in becoming whole and healing.

Shange covers many black feminist issues through the characters. Shange's choreopoem is one of the first performance pieces to deal explicitly with what we now call "date rape," acknowledging in the mid-1970s that rape is most likely experienced not as assault by a stranger, but rather as assault by an acquaintance. Her poem "latent rapists" captures the isolation and pain of betrayal and violence that women experience as a result of being raped, while making it clear that rape is a violent act that is not isolated to alleys and is not the fault of the woman who survives the attack.

Several of Shange's poems challenge the notion of black women's sexual availability and sexuality. "sechita" and "orange butterflies" reveal the efforts of women who are perceived by men as sexual wantons to come to terms with their oppression and find ways to honor themselves. The three women who "share" one man look not to him but to each other, divorcing themselves from the competition over men that divides them. The "ladies" reveal inner strength to resist definition by men, and to resist abuse by men. Ultimately, it is only through loving god in themselves that they can become complete, whole, and ready for positive relationships.

The most controversial poem is the Lady in Red's "A Nite with Beau Willie Brown"; in it, Beau Willie and Crystal struggle with each other because they cannot fight the institutionalized racism and sexism that plague their lives. Beau Willie is a Vietnam Veteran; he experiences post-traumatic stress disorder (marked by his flashbacks and his use of alcohol), is unable to read, and works in a dead-end job as a cabbie. Crystal has been his "girl since she was fourteen / when he caught her on the stairs"; she has two children by Beau Willie. She has left him because of his continued physical abuse of her, and Beau desperately wants to have his "family." Their struggle includes one incident when Beau beat Crystal with a high chair (while the baby, Kwame, was still sitting in it). Beau ultimately forces his way into Crystal's apartment, and in an effort to get her to agree to marry him, drops the children out the window. Crystal's circumstances contribute to their conflict; from her early sexual relationship with Beau Willie to the fact that when "beau willie oozed kindness & crystal who had known so lil / let beau hold kwame/" (Shange 59), her life is one example of devalued black womanhood.

Any work that diverged from the black nationalist aesthetic popular at the time, which "discouraged any literary exploration of gender and other differences that might complicate a unitary conception of the black experience," was challenged (Dubey 1). As Dubey explains, "Their desire to assert an intimate and symbiotic connection between art and ideology motivated the Black Aestheticians' conception of literature as a direct reflection of social and cultural experience" (9). Shange's work clearly builds on the criticism inherent in Childress's *Wine in the Wilderness*, with its opposition to a sexist nationalist philosophy. Shange succeeds in inscribing a new black female subjectivity, one that is multivalent and *not* an essentialist "THE black woman." While the women share some experiences, they are individuated by their specific experiences. Shange also plays with form, invoking a ritual format with elements of African dance and African diaspora music (jazz, R&B) and call-and-response form. Shange's courage to critique the sexism of the nationalist aesthetic facilitated the writing—and production—of plays like Aishah Rahman's *Unfinished Women Cry in No Man's Land While a*

Bird Dies in a Gilded Cage (1977), Alexis DeVeaux's *The Tapestry* (1976), and P. J. Gibson's *Brown Silk and Magenta Sunsets* (1985).

The emergent black feminism of the 1970s and '80s marks the intersection between the Women's Liberation Movement and the Civil Rights Movement, but also diverges from them. Particularly, black feminists were less interested in the right to work (because the majority of black women had long worked outside the home), but rather were concerned with issues of maintaining relationships with black men within families, liberation from the negative images of black women (particularly that of the sexually available, promiscuous black woman), acceptance for black lesbians and gay men in black communities, and inclusion in the word "woman." Concurrently, black women writers like Michelle Wallace and Audre Lorde explored the construction of women under black nationalism and worked to redefine that construction. The emergence of writers like Toni Morrison and Alice Walker and the rise in the numbers of black women literary critics enabled the emergence of black feminist literary criticism.

Jacqueline Bobo writes that "two significant purposes are key in Black feminist criticism: to intervene strategically in privileged discourses that attempt to undervalue the merits of Black women's creative work; and to advance the causes of Black women and those of others at risk of oppression" (Bobo xviii). The black female scholars whose work establishes black feminist work did not come to their understandings of the intersections of race, class, and gender by accident. Rather, they knew the long history of black women's political, social, and artistic activism; it informed and fortified their work. Barbara Smith writes in her essay "Toward a Black Feminist Criticism," in *The Truth that Never Hurts: Writings on Race, Gender, and Freedom,* "at the present time I feel that the politics of feminism have a direct relationship to the state of Black women's literature. A viable, autonomous Black feminist movement in this country would open up the space needed for the exploration of Black women's lives and the creation of a consciously Black woman-identified art" (5). These two concepts-plus the exploration of black women's lives and the creation of a consciously black woman-identified art—stand as the key elements in black feminist aesthetics. Several years later, Barbara Christian would broaden black feminist criticism; in "But What Do We Think We're Doing Anyway?" Christian suggests that we read "the works of the writers, in order to understand their ramifications" (72).

Although black feminist critics explored and defined black feminist literature, theatre history and criticism would not make the same kinds of strides. While there were sometimes plays by black women playwrights included in anthologies, there was not a black feminist theatre criticism that grew parallel to that of literary criticism. In part this is because of the small numbers of black women who were, and are, involved in academic theatre and criticism; the majority of black women involved in theatre have been practitioners rather than scholars. Few black women theatre scholars' work is explicitly *feminist*, and only now are we gaining a body of black feminist critical work on black feminist drama.

There is, of course, a body of feminist criticism of black feminist drama. The more obviously feminist plays, like *for colored girls,* have been the subject of many feminist analyses. But because black feminism is constituted differently, and manifests differently, the feminism inherent in the works of black women is sometimes missed. For example, in Sue-Ellen Case's 1988 *Feminism and Theatre,* one of the founding works of feminist dramatic criticism, she comments that "though [Adrienne] Kennedy's plays are not explicitly feminist, her leading female characters situate the effects of racism within a female subject" (102). A black feminist analysis of Kennedy's work reveals that she cannot separate the effects of racism and sexism; characters such as Sarah in *Funnyhouse of a Negro* are in their predicaments precisely because of their race *and* sex. In other words, Kennedy does not just create black characters; she creates black *female* characters who struggle with their sex and race. Though Case did not see evidence of a "black feminist theatre movement" in the late 1980s, it was there; it just did not look like the feminist theatre she knew (105). While feminist theatre criticism and theory grew, black feminist criticism and theory remained the interest of a few scholars.[2]

The Realization of a Black Feminist Aesthetic

Since 1990, there has been an impressive increase in dramas written by black women, many of which I consider black feminist. There has been a simultaneous evolution of black feminist scholarship in all areas, from film to sociology to health. The strong development of black feminist theory and the emergence of womanist theory have enabled the development of a black feminist aesthetic.

In developing this aesthetic, I have drawn on a range of black feminisms, from the black lesbian feminism of Audre Lorde and Barbara Smith to the womanism of Alice Walker. In drawing from these diverse theories, I am working toward a broad, rather than narrow, concept of a black feminist aesthetic. This aesthetic is grounded in the feminism of black women since the nineteenth century, but has broadened with the times. It still maintains its focus on the lives of black women in U.S. culture. It also continues to be concerned with the images of black women in the popular imagination as well as in popular culture. It embraces the history of black women in the United States, Africa, and the rest of the diaspora, and seeks to recover and remember our foremothers. It is critical of violence against women, and critical of black men when necessary. It works to expose homophobia wherever it may reside. It is at times nationalist, and separatist, or both, or neither.[3]

Contemporary black feminism is interested in investigating the intersections of race, gender, class, orientation, and other locations and identities. Although it is woman-centered, it does not exclude men. As Sherley Anne Williams stressed, it should, and does, "do more than merely focus on how black men have treated black women in literature" (69). It is committed to, as Alice Walker said, "survival and wholeness of entire people, male *and* female" (370). As Freda Scott Giles states:

> Womanist theatre inscribes and incorporates these features, including those described as Afrocentric: for instance, the view of time as circular rather than linear; the retention of rhythmic, rhetorical, and musical traditions from African ritual theatre; and the blurring of the separation between performer and audience. The rebellious and irreverent use of the language of the colonizer to forge a cultural identity for the colonized, the re-visioning of Eurocentric and Afrocentric imagery and symbolism, and the subversion of the Western idea of genre, major precepts of post-Afrocentric dramatic theory, also significantly are present in womanist drama. (Giles 1996–97)

Having "grown up" with the larger feminist movement, young black feminists today have woven black feminism into their lives without it necessarily being a conscious feminism. Contemporary black feminism—more accurately, feminism*s*—undermine the "facile dualisms or binary oppositions of class, race, and sex" (Wallace 63). Joan Morgan describes her feminism as one that "places the welfare of black women and the black community on its list of priorities" (70–71).

It is not unreasonable to look for or to see black feminism in contemporary drama. As Barbara Christian explained, "It is often in the poem, the story, the play, rather than in Western philosophical theorizing, that feminist thought / feeling evolves, challenges and renews itself" ("Highs and Lows" 49). In the following chapters, we will explore the artistic and political breadth of contemporary black feminist playwriting, the issues of contemporary black women playwrights, and the aesthetics that make them something we can call black feminist.

In chapter 2, I explore the plays of Pearl Cleage; she shares with Clarke and Dickerson the experience of the second wave of feminism. Cleage's plays make explicit the intersections of race, gender, and sexuality while entertaining her audience with interesting, complex characters. Cleage's politics, like those of the other women whose works are investigated here, emerge through her art. In Cleage's case, she uses traditional well-made play structure and melodrama, and reveals the issues of concern through character dialogue (seldom do the characters speak in monologues in her full-length plays; they do in her one-acts).

In chapter 3, I delve in depth into Breena Clarke and Glenda Dickerson's play *Re/Membering Aunt Jemima*. As an icon that has incredible negative resonance for black Americans, Aunt Jemima has a sordid history. Clarke and Dickerson use this icon to examine the history of black women, in its ignominy and its glory. Their incorporation of both historical and cultural characters reveals some of the complexity of black womanhood in the United States.

Chapter 4, takes up the work of Suzan-Lori Parks, the most celebrated of the contemporary black women playwrights. Parks's work is complex; she engages the images and stereotypes of black men and women, and attempts to reveal their inaccuracy. This is particularly true of her earlier work; in this chapter, I explore both *Death of the Last Black Man in the Whole Entire World* and *Venus: A Play*. These two plays are important for the ways in which they use images, stereotypes, and history in order to reveal a critique of U.S. culture, particularly popular and academic cultures. In addition, Parks's more recent play *In The Blood* is examined for its look into the tragic victimization of a young black welfare mother.

The fifth chapter takes up the work of Kia Corthron, a young playwright whose works are gaining in popularity, particularly her play *Breath, Boom*. I consider four of her plays: *Wake Up, Lou Riser; Splash Hatch on the E Going Down; Breath, Boom;* and *Come Down Burning*. All of these plays take up issues of social justice and share theoretical groundings with critical race feminism. Corthron's investigations into manifestations of issues such as teen pregnancy, abortion, racist violence, and gang violence offer a black feminist perspective on these issues. Her plays contain both staged and retold violence, and implicate the audience in the lives of her characters.

In the sixth chapter, I consider two plays that engage the issues of black lesbian history and visibility. *A Lady and a Woman,* by Shirlene Holmes, and *blood pudding,* by Sharon Bridgforth, highlight the histories of black lesbians within specifically black communities. Their "speculative fictions" fill a largely empty space in representations of black women, specifically lesbians, and specifically representations of black lesbians that do not denigrate their experiences. By taking black lesbians as the subject of their plays, Holmes and Bridgforth also create representations of black female sexuality that do not rely on old, negative stereotypes.

Finally, I sketch out something that I might call a black feminist aesthetic. By aesthetic, I mean not necessarily the "beauty" of a text, but rather the elements of the text or performance that invoke a particular history, politics, and philosophy of a "community" (broadly construed). The elements of the text or performance that comprise the aesthetic run the range from structure, to plot, to characters. The central questions about such an aesthetic are whether or not the text critiques, shifts, or alters representations from dominant culture stereotype, and whether or not the text is structurally consistent with the goals of the "community." An aesthetic should also conceive of the function of art. In other words, is it the responsibility of the artist to address issues of social and political importance? Or is the function of art only entertainment, or the creation of a technically "perfect play?" In addition to the concerns of the community socially, to what extent is artistic innovation important? By engaging in this project, I have attempted to begin to fill a gap in feminist theory and criticism of drama and performance. By looking to dramatic literature, I hope to uncover what "black feminist drama" has looked like, and what it looks like at the beginning of the new century.

Pearl Cleage's Black Feminism

Of all of the playwrights whose work I explore in this book, Cleage's are the most explicitly recognizable as feminist. I should emphasize that these playwrights are all, in their way, feminist, but Pearl Cleage's work is artistic and political and explicitly from a black feminist perspective. For Cleage, there is never a moment when she is not conscious of being both black and female, when she is not fighting against both sexism and racism. Each of her plays combines struggles against racism and sexism; she uses specific historical moments to engage her audience in a moment in black history.

In fact, her essay/performance piece *Mad at Miles* provides us with a clear delineation of her black feminism. "I am writing to expose and explore the point where racism and sexism meet. I am writing to help myself understand the full effects of being black and female in a culture that is both racist and sexist" (4). For Cleage, "A lot of my work is committed to saying out loud what people have said to me, so that the ones who have been abused can say, 'Thank God. I thought I was the only person who this happened to'" (Greene 53). Cleage is fully engaged in the ongoing struggle for liberation from racism and sexism and their corollary "isms," including homophobia.

In this chapter, I will explore the issues Cleage places in the center of her plays: violence against women/domestic violence, abortion/reproductive rights, depression and post-traumatic stress, drug addiction, parenting, and prostitution. In addition to these issues, Cleage reimagines specific historical moments: the Exodus of 1879, the Harlem Renaissance, and the Civil Rights Movement. Each of these time periods figures into her plays not only because of the racial issues they encompass, but also because of the issues for women that occur simultaneously. Inspired by Barbara Christian's suggestion of letting the work generate the theory, I will use

Cleage's feminism to structure my analysis, and that analysis will include the importance of the relationships between the struggles against racism and sexism.

Escaping Violence by *Flyin' West*

The violence faced by the women in *Flyin' West* is twofold: they are threatened by violence because of both their race and their sex. When I first read this play, I was frustrated that Cleage complicated the story of the "Exodusters" with a plot about domestic violence—or the opposite, that a story about domestic violence was complicated with the important historical moment of the Exodus of 1879. Reading the play from a black feminist perspective, however, reveals the play's logic. Of course these two issues should exist in the same play. Cleage marks the intersection of sexism and racism by drawing on this historical moment.

In 1879, in response to the increased violence against blacks at the end of Reconstruction, at least fifty thousand blacks left Louisiana, Mississippi, and other southern states to homestead in Kansas and other western states. The "Exoduster" movement was spurred by a committee of blacks who included Benjamin Singleton, head of the Tennessee Real Estate and Homestead Association, and Henry Adams, a U.S. Army veteran. These "Exodusters" escaped a South renewed by the withdrawal of U.S. troops from southern cities; blacks were subject to violence, lack of educational facilities, rape and assault of black women, and a system of peonage that rivaled slavery.

Cleage is emphatically interested in the issue of domestic violence, especially the domestic violence experienced by black women. Racism, she observes, is easy for black men and women to fight. Sexism, on the other hand, is deferred as unimportant or less important than the struggle against racism. As a black feminist, Cleage sees these issues as two sides of the same coin, both as manifestations of a system that is simultaneously racist, sexist, and homophobic, one in which power is held by white men. She embodies this intersection in Frank, Minnie's abusive husband. Frank's abuse is connected to the racist violence that the "sisters" have escaped by packing up and moving to Nicodemus. Their moving from Memphis was prompted by a desire to not only be free, but to avoid the inherent difficulties of living among whites; when living near (because "among" was not really the case), it was clear that blacks would work for whites, not for themselves. Their "inferiority" was assumed. In Nicodemus, on the other hand, blacks wielded power among themselves and ultimately are able to triumph over the prospectors who have come to buy their land.

It is easy to see Frank as the completely evil character in this "melo-drama."[1] In fact, as Sullivan notes, one critic describes the play as "no more than a domestic potboiler with all the subtlety of a bad Boucicault melo-drama" (12). As an audience, we sympathize with Sophie, Fannie, and Miss Leah; they are the heroines of the play, they are the ones who speak for Cleage, demonstrating black feminist values. Miss Leah asserts her knowl-edge as the elder of the group by her stories of slavery and comments like "Colored men always tryin' to tell you how to do somethin' even if you been doin' it longer than they been peein' standin' up" (10). We are attracted to Miss Leah's independence and her courage and strength to survive through slavery and Reconstruction, and encouraged by her determination to home-stead in Kansas. Fannie supplies tales of her politically active family, of "the literary societies and the Sunday socials and the forums. Mama and Daddy's house was always full of people talking at the top of their lungs about the best way to save the race" (23). Sophie fiercely maintains her independence from anyone who would try to control her, whether it be black man or white. She is also committed to the community and to maintaining black control of Nicodemus. She is, in many ways, a black nationalist (in the contemporary sense of the word, rather than the 1960s sense of the word, that is, someone who is committed to seeing black people survive and thrive); she creates a plan for the community and defends her "sister" Min from Frank's violence. She succeeds in driving the white speculators out of Nicodemus, making it possible for the town to remain under black control.

It is therefore easy to see the women as the heroines of the play. If one sets Wil against Frank, it is also possible to see the two men in stark contrast to each other. It is almost as if Cleage gives us Wil to ensure that she will not be accused of not representing a "good black man." Wil is emphati-cally not an abuser of women; rather, he believes that "a colored women is a precious jewel deserving of my respect, my love and my protection" (17). He is gallant and does not "understand how a colored man can hit a colored woman. . . . We been through too much together" (72). There is certainly idealism in Wil; he is exactly the kind of man Cleage thinks more black men should be. Frank, clearly, is not.

Not insignificantly, Cleage's "bad guy" is a mulatto: he is a tragic mu-latto.[2] Frank is a "bad guy" because we see him hit Min, try to coerce her into selling her portion of the family's land, and because, I think, he hates Nicodemus. The deeper part of understanding Frank, though, requires an understanding of history and a knowledge of African American literature's legacy, of which Cleage sees herself a part. The source of Frank's anger, of his "badness," lies precisely in his history and his heritage, and the fact that he lives as a "mulatto" in a racist and sexist culture. It is easy to simply identify Frank as an evil man because he beats and demeans Minnie. But Cleage is giving us something else here, something more subtle. Frank is enamored with whiteness and white culture, and is particularly proud of his ability to pass for white. He also hates his own blackness, evidenced by his actions and statements. When Minnie reveals that she and Frank have white friends in London, it comes as a surprise to the other women. "Frank says he doesn't see why he only has to be with Negroes since he has as much white blood in him as colored," Minnie relates (34). Later at dinner, Frank himself says "To tell you the truth, I've seen about all the Negroes I need to see in this life," after Miss Leah asks him if he ever misses seeing other people like himself (42).

Frank's narrative is derived from the classic narratives of tragic mulattos as imagined by other black writers; he particularly reminds me of Langston Hughes's character Bert in *Mulatto*. Like Frank, Bert is the bastard son of a white man who would not, or could not, marry his mother. Frank is supported by his father, as is Hughes's Bert, but never really acknowledged as such or brought into the family; he is always an outsider. Frank acutely feels his "inferiority" to his white relatives because they continually remind him of his half-blackness. Bert thinks that his half-whiteness entitles him to at least some of the power and privilege of being a white man, as does Frank. When he receives the telegram telling him that his parentage cannot be proven and that he will not be receiving any of his father's estate, Frank is distraught and angry.

For Cleage, as a black feminist, Frank's conflicted relationship with whiteness and white culture in his racist world generates the vicious anger that we see him take out on his darker wife. Cleage examines this dynamic in her essay "Basic Training: The Beginnings of Wisdom." As she states:

> Although all African American insanity, male and female, can ultimately be explained by the long ago presence of the slave ships pulling up on the coast of Africa, that blood soaked presence cannot continue to be an acceptable reason for our current sorry state. We cannot undo slavery. It happened. We cannot ignore racism. It is a fact of our lives. [. . .] There is no white man physically present in the house when a black man decides to beat his wife. There is no white man present when black men prey on women old enough to be their grandmothers to get money for crack. There is no white man present when black girls are not safe from rape in their own neighborhoods or in their own front rooms. [. . .] And, *yes,* I really do understand that white men are responsible for the madness, but who is responsible for the cure? (36–37)

Cleage does not deny the adverse effects of slavery and racism on blacks, but she refuses to allow slavery to be responsible for the continuation of violence against women or the continuation of sexism. Racism cannot eclipse sexism, because both exist simultaneously; that fact is felt acutely by black women, even while it is ignored by black men. The fact that racism affects black men does not mean that racism does not also affect black women; racism cannot be an excuse for violence against black women (or black men, for that matter).

Frank's self-hatred arises from his status as a biracial black man (even while he may pass for white) in a white supremacist society. He cannot love the black part of himself; he wants to erase his blackness and avoids contact with other blacks as much as possible. His move to England was precipitated by his desire to be able to be someone new in a new place, one where U.S. attitudes and slavery did not exist. As a black American expatriate, he is able to find a measure of acceptance in white society that will be difficult for him to find and maintain in the United States. His marriage to Minnie, who is obviously black, is somewhat acceptable in England, while most states in the United States still have antimiscegenation laws. As long as he is passing for white, antimiscegenation laws would prohibit him from presenting himself to whites in the United States as married to Minnie. As Minnie relates to her sisters, "He isn't used to being treated like other colored people. He gets so angry when we have to get on the Jim Crow car. When we can't go into the restaurants. I think if Frank had to live here, he might go mad" (49). Mad, indeed; he would certainly begin to suffer from being treated like a black person, particularly when he does not believe that he should be treated as one. He cannot pretend to be a white man married to a black woman, and when he first met Minnie, he could not pretend to be white. He tells Minnie, "Things were going fine [with his gambling with white men in town] until one of them asked me about the nigger woman who kept following me around the train. I laughed it off, but my luck changed after that so I know they suspected something. But I should have known better than to depend on you for luck. You're too black to bring me any good luck. All you got to give is misery. Pure D misery and little black pickaninnies just like you" (55). His vitriol is so clear here, and it is generated specifically by losing money in a poker game to white men. He has interpreted his change in luck as directly related to blackness, Minnie's specifically, which has in return "contaminated" him. The sisters' conversations about Frank also demonstrate Cleage's construction of him. Sophie says "I think Frank hates being colored. I don't understand Negroes like that"; Sophie sees evidence by what Frank says and does that he is deeply entrenched in self-hate (54).

Minnie's comment that "Frank says he doesn't see why he only has to be with Negroes since he has as much white blood in him as colored" is further evidence of Frank's self-hatred and antiblack racism. Frank embodies the male version of the "tragic mulatto"; he is determined that he should be given preferential treatment because of his partial whiteness and refuses to see himself as part of a larger black community. The opposite of such a "tragic" mulatto is someone like Sophie who, while she has one white parent, clearly identifies herself as black and is most comfortable within a black community. This is and is not a gender difference; it is possible for a "mulatto" to be "tragic" or not. In other words, part of what makes the "tragic" nature of the "tragic mulatta/o" is his or her acceptance of his or her blackness, and the degree to which he or she is willing to turn his or her back on her community for his or her own sake or profit. Frank's desire to sell Minnie's share of the homestead to white prospectors represents a traitor position, for he is willing to destroy the all-black town of Nicodemus for his own benefit (that is money on which to live abroad after he has been disinherited).

Frank's self-hatred and hatred of blackness is directly connected to his abuse of Minnie. In spite of his self-hatred, Frank did indeed marry Minnie. He is initially attracted to her at the conservatory because he hears her singing Puccini; he assumes that her knowledge of classical music is a sign that she is as assimilated as he. They had only known each other a few weeks before marrying. Cleage constructs an abusive relationship clearly and accurately. Frank's outbursts against Minnie are often connected to her doing something that is "black"; for example, he angers quickly when Minnie has had Miss Leah braid her hair. He pushes her to the floor after he loses money in the poker game. His abuse of Minnie increases with her pregnancy. "When his father died and his brothers stopped sending money, it just got worse and worse. It was almost like he couldn't stand to look at me," says Minnie, defending Frank's increasing violence. He beats her the worst after hearing that his claim for some of his father's estate has been denied. Each time, he makes up with Minnie, trying to excuse his abuse by claiming that he "has a bad temper sometimes" (67).

This scenario reflects the difficult position of African American women wanting to protect their community against racist violence but also wanting to speak out against sexist violence within it. As is true with batterers, "power and control are at the root of the domestic violence that leaves as many as 4 million women a year battered by men who say they love them" (Briggs and Davis). The problem is even more serious for black women, who are most often killed by acquaintances or family members. In their article, Briggs and Davis interview Pearl Cleage, who comments that "there's no widespread agreement in the Black community that it's even a crime to hit a woman. We see the problem, but when you articulate it to people they say, 'Oh, you don't understand the pressure of the brother. You're a male-basher.'" There is heavy resistance to bringing up or challenging domestic violence; "shining a light on the abuse of Black women is often seen as adding fuel to the fires of racist stereotypes" (Briggs and Davis). One example of this is a review of *Flyin' West* in the *New York Amsterdam News.* The author describes the plot of the play as "four Black women and a man, domiciled in a predominantly Black township in Nicodemus, Kansas, are willing to die to maintain ownership, control, and protection of their land" (10). Nowhere in the entire review is there a mention of Frank's abuse of Minnie; in fact, Frank is described as Minnie's "elitist mulatto husband" (10). Certainly, Frank is an elitist mulatto, but he is also abusing his wife. There is a theoretical tug-of-war between two divergent perspectives. Some believe that emasculation of black men is the largest problem, and if black men regain their masculinity by beating black women, well, black women should just accept that for the good of the race. For others, violence is a problem in and of itself and should not be excused because of racism.

Frank's demise is not unlike that of other abusers whose female partners feel the only way out of the abusive situation is to kill the batterer. Generally, black women are less inclined to use social services or police because of their long history of mistrusting the system. As Cleage says, "The Black churches are still largely controlled by conservative Black men. We don't have a huge progressive wing of any denomination. What the church tends to do is counsel the woman to go back home and try harder. To encourage them to come to church and try to get their husbands to come to church, but not specifically to look at the problem of sexist violence against women" (Briggs and Davis). Fortunately for Minnie, she is surrounded by a family who supports her and will not stand by and allow her to be beaten and abused by Frank.

The choice of melodrama for this play is thought-provoking. *Flyin' West* clearly follows in a tradition, but which one? While one might be tempted to compare it to Dion Boucicault's *The Octoroon,* there are stark and significant differences that distinguish Boucicault's play from African American literature. Melodrama exists as a trope in African American literature, including drama, from the slave narrative to contemporary works like Cleage's. As Sullivan correctly notes, "it is to say that African American writers may have a particular stake in re-presenting or revising this genre [melodrama], which is so imbued with color" (18). Melodrama as a choice of genre also marks Cleage's plays as accessible to her audiences. Melodrama is familiar to most audiences; it relies on a few conventions that are instantly recognizable. First, melodrama relies on "good" and "bad" characters. The conflict between the characters represents the conflict between "good" and "evil." Sometimes evil triumphs, but not always. Second, melodrama typically reflects storytelling, which enhances its accessibility. The single-set staging of melodrama enables a focus of dramatic action on the "family" and the obstacles they must overcome.

The consequences of passing and despising your own race are death and destruction; the "tragic mulatto" who refuses a connection with his own community can only die. Langston Hughes's *Mulatto*'s melodrama arises from the same essential inequity of racism that *Flyin' West*'s does, like the melodrama of *Celia, A Slave*, or *Incidents in the Life of a Slave Girl*. The fights against racism and sexism need the melodramatic clarity of "good" and "bad" to provide clarity for the audience. Still, Cleage does not leave her melodrama uncomplicated; we have to move to understanding that Frank is not "bad" because he is a man, but that his encounters with racism do not excuse his treatment of Minnie.

Women's Blues: Love, Sex, and Murder in Harlem

The transition from the relative prosperity of and investment in the black community of Harlem in the 1920s to the harsh, lean years of the Depression provides Cleage with an ideal setting to excavate the changes facing African Americans. The Depression accelerated the Great Migration, where millions of rural black southerners moved north to find work in cities. Unfortunately, opportunities were not significantly better in Harlem or any other northern city. In Harlem, the retreat of rich white patrons slowed the production of fine art and literature; the trickle of prosperity that reached the denizens of Harlem dried up, as did regular jobs. Poverty hit Harlem hard.

The attendant difficulties of blacks in 1930s Harlem are embodied in the characters of *Blues for an Alabama Sky*. Angel is out of work, partially because of her public, drunken response to her Italian mobster boyfriend/ boss. Though as a singer she might have been able to find other work, the white crowds are no longer flocking to Harlem, and there are no opportunities left for her. Her "brother" Guy, a costume designer, wishes to leave Harlem and join Josephine Baker in Paris, where he would be able to continue to work. Sam, the doctor, lives with the frustration of working at Harlem Hospital, where he sees too many women and children adversely affected by poverty. Delia hopes that she can alleviate some of that suffering by introducing birth control and family planning to Harlem. Leland has just come to Harlem from Alabama and is out of sync with the urban, cosmopolitan world in which he finds himself. All of them, in some way, accentuate the ways in which the Depression affected blacks. Some of the ways in which life in Harlem has become hard show up in comments by Angel: "I've been all over Harlem and nobody will even give me the time of day. There aren't any jobs doing anything, especially singing for your supper. Whole families sitting on the sidewalk with their stuff set out beside them. No place to sleep. No place to wash. Walking all day" (117). Harlem has changed from the promised land to a desolate wasteland.

Leland's naïveté intersects most importantly with the lives of Sam, Delia, and Angel. In Angel, Leland sees the replacement for his wife, who died in childbirth. It is important that she died in childbirth, because it highlights one of the problems of rural poverty and the lack of medical care. Angel also sees her salvation through Leland; after she is abandoned by her lover, she must find another man in order to feel that she is important and to have someone who would, or could, support her financially. While Angel feels she needs a man, her values are not "traditional," and she is not looking for a life as a wife and mother. If anything, she is much more likely to want to go to Paris with Guy, should he be able to convince Josephine Baker that she should hire him as her costumer. As Freda Scott Giles says, "Angel, however, can only see her destiny in terms of the economic and emotional support of a man, and uses her body as the commodity through which she will achieve this support" (710). Angel thinks that she desires to be a "free woman" like her image of Baker, but she refuses to consider learning to type in order to get a job. She has become accustomed to using her body for her survival. While she massages Delia's head, she reveals that "When I was working at Miss Lillie's, as many of those old men would pay me for this as would pay me for the other" (124). Being a prostitute was a way of surviving, and now Angel knows of no other way to live. She gives up the opportunity to go to Paris by becoming pregnant with Leland's child (89).

Angel's pregnancy is the intersection of the other explicitly feminist issue in the play, where Sam and Delia's lives are affected. The first time we meet Sam, he relates the difficulties of his job:

> SAM: They didn't even know she was carrying twins and one of them was coming breech. When I let her husband know what the risks were, he broke down and cried. He kept saying, "That's the best woman in the world in there, Doc. That's the best woman in the world."
> DELIA: If she's so precious to him, why didn't he take her to the doctor?
> SAM: He did. He just took her a little late, that's all.
> DELIA: Why didn't she take herself? If she's old enough to have two babies at one time, she ought to be able to figure out how to catch the subway (109).

Without proper care, childbirth can be dangerous. Certainly, we saw the issue of birth control as an important issue for the women writers of the

Harlem Renaissance; of particular concern was the lack of adequate medical care for pregnant women, the toll of repeated pregnancies, and the potential danger of childbirth to both mother and child. While Angelina Weld Grimké, one of the Renaissance feminists, advocated not having children at all, many of them were concerned with families being able to plan when to have children and how many children to have. Their concern was in having a black population that could support itself and be healthy, which was all but impossible without access to birth control. As Delia says, "I'm just trying to give women in Harlem a chance to plan their families" (112).

The issue of birth control is not an easy one. This exchange between Sam and Delia highlights the difficulty of Delia's work:

> SAM: I deliver babies everyday to exhausted women and stone-broke men, but they never ask me about birth control. They ask me about jobs.
>
> DELIA: What does that mean?
>
> SAM: It means we still see our best hope in the faces of our children and it's going to take more than some rich white women playing missionary in Harlem to convince these Negroes otherwise.
>
> DELIA: Why can't we take help wherever we can find it?
>
> SAM: Because it's more complicated than that. The Garveyites are already charging genocide and the clinic isn't even open yet. (130)

The nationalist charge of genocide is not new in the 1930s (or even in 2004), but Delia sees the issue much differently. It is more important to her, as it was to the Renaissance feminists, that women and men have the right to limit the number of children they have. Certainly slave women used herbal birth control methods and herbal abortifacients to avoid having children they did not want to see sold away from them. It was easier and less dangerous than having the child and then having to kill it, as also happened.[3]

Sam also performs abortions. At this point, of course, to do so is illegal. While Sam seems to criticize Delia's "revolution," he clearly understands that some of the problems he sees as a doctor would be alleviated by the availability of birth control to the community. He is not ashamed of providing abortions to women who need them; after all, as a physician, he is trained to do them correctly, and the women are much less likely to die as a result.

The conflict that emerges around Angel's pregnancy and abortion reveals the differences between the urban and the rural, but also the differences between different kinds of black folks. For Angel, aborting the pregnancy is not much of a question; she understands that she really does not love Leland, and realizes that the opportunity before her, to go to Paris, is much more enticing than marrying Leland. The fact that she tells Leland she is pregnant is predicated on the idea that he is her "last hope" for the emotional and economic support of a man, even though Leland is new to Harlem. It is partially in response to seeing the eviction notice on the door of the apartment she shares with Guy:

ANGEL: I was hoping you'd come.
LELAND: You were?
ANGEL: Yes. I want your son to grow up with his father.
LELAND: What did you say?
ANGEL: We're going to have a child.
LELAND: Are you sure?
ANGEL: I'm sure.

There is a resignation in her tone; she is not thrilled about the pregnancy. In her earlier conversation with Sam, he tells her he is "sorry this isn't what you want," and she responds, "Yeah. Me too" (165). It is only out of desperation that she even tells Leland that she is pregnant.

When Guy gets his telegram from Josephine, there is quite suddenly another possibility for Angel, one that does not require marrying the "country" Leland. At this point, she has already told him that she is pregnant. She does not love him, and she initially plans to tell him that she had a miscarriage. Sam thinks losing both Angel and the baby will kill Leland, but Angel responds, "No, it won't! He'll live though it just fine. And so will I. This is my chance to live free, Doc, and I'm taking it" (175). Sam is hesitant; though he was willing to abort Angel's earlier pregnancy by her Italian mobster, this one is different. This pregnancy involves the aborting of a child that one of the parents—Leland—wants. He ultimately agrees, though, setting in motion the series of events that will destroy four lives.

Leland shows up at Angel's apartment just after she has returned from Sam's office. Angel is careless in telling him that their relationship is over. She tries to make excuses for her trip to Paris with Guy, but Leland is not buying it; Angel grows so frustrated, she simply tells him the truth. "Listen to me, Alabama. This isn't about you and it isn't about all the dead mamas and all the dead babies and all the things that are supposed to move me. I'm not that kind of colored woman! I just don't want to think about all that anymore" (180). Leland, of course, is incredulous; after all, he has believed the line Angel has been feeding him about being in love with him. When she reveals that she "got rid of it," Leland flies into a rage (180). "You got rid of my son? How . . . Dr. Thomas? You let Dr. Thomas take my son? (*He grabs her by the shoulders as if to shake her, but stops himself and releases her.*) If you didn't have Anna's face, I'd kill you," he replies, and storms out of the apartment (180). He does not kill Angel; instead, he kills Sam, who he meets in the hallway.

While we might be tempted to sympathize with Leland, his conservative values are not those of the other characters, and Cleage has deliberately constructed him as a character we cannot help but see as naive and out of sync with the rest of the characters. Sam, Delia, Guy, and Angel live in the world of the present and future, while Leland lives in the past. Leland's ideas are archaic, and we can see the connection between his sexism ("the cure for mothers who don't want babies is fathers who do") and his homophobia ("Don't put God's name in the stuff you're talking about! I don't know how sophisticated New York people feel about it [homosexuality], but in Alabama, there's still such a thing as abomination") (155, 158). As an audience, we are charmed by Guy and are appalled by Leland's homophobic reaction to Guy's sexuality. None of the other characters has a problem with Guy's gayness; Cleage implies that Guy is not alone as a gay man during the Renaissance. The world of the gay Renaissance includes Bruce Nugent and other artists, including perhaps Langston Hughes. After all, as Guy says, "when we first got to Harlem, we specialized in gowns for discriminating gentlemen. Don't look so shocked, Deal. You don't think these six-foot queens buy off the rack, do you" (142)?

Working against homophobia is also clearly a black feminist struggle, one that is important but is not always engaged explicitly. Cleage, though, has no qualms about addressing homophobia. In fact, her construction of Leland clearly associates sexism and homophobia. His views about women and homosexuality are cut from the same cloth; they both rely on a conservative interpretation of the Bible that is out of place in the New York City of the Renaissance. This is the Harlem of Adam Clayton Powell, where much of the focus of church is on making life better in the present instead of focusing on the afterlife. This is a church willing to take up the issue of birth control for the benefit of the community; birth control offers a way to help families survive, especially in hard economic times. While the church's preference might be to continue to proscribe against it, longer-term survival of the race necessitated ensuring the health of women and children.

Surprisingly, even black audiences respond positively to Guy. Cleage was curious about how audiences would react to Guy; as will be discussed in chapter 6, homophobia is more typical of black communities that are conservative. In fact, many of the most conservative contemporary blacks have views similar to those of Leland; in criticizing him, Cleage is not subtly critiquing that contemporary conservative bent in various black communities. In creating Guy, Cleage creates a gay man who is clearly and simply out of the closet and unapologetic for his sexuality. Cleage says:

Fig. 1. Cherise Boothe and Darryl Theirse in *Blues for an Alabama Sky*, Berkshire
Theatre Festival, 2004. Photo by Kevin Sprague.

Fig. 2. Rachel Leslie and Shane Taylor in *Blues for an Alabama Sky*, Berkshire Theatre Festival, 2004. Photo by Kevin Sprague.

I know there is homophobia in the country generally, and especially within the black community. So I was very curious about how audiences would respond, not only because Guy is gay, but because he has no angst about it—he is not closeted, he's not scared, he carries a straight razor. He is completely the opposite of the tormented gay character that we know is going to die in the end. When Blues opened in Atlanta, I was really happy that people responded so enthusiastically to him. It's wonderful to look at people in the audience whom I know have a lot of homophobia in their daily lives cheering and saying, "Go on, brother!" to a guy on the stage, where they probably would be very nervous to do that in real life. (Langworthy 22)

Guy emerges as a whole character, not as a caricature of black gay men.

It is also interesting that Cleage chooses to create in Angel a black woman who is not the "superwoman" or even the perfect role model. There has been a tendency, as Trudier Harris so cogently explains in her book *Mothers, Sinners, and Saints,* for black women to be portrayed in works by black feminists as women who are often "saints," setting an example of an ideal of black womanhood. It is often a sacrificing mother who will do anything for her children and her man; she is the glue that holds the community together. Angel is none of these. She rejects the concept of motherhood and desires a selfish freedom that has little or nothing to do with anyone else. After Guy tells her at Miss Lillie's that he is also saving money to escape a life of prostitution, Angel does not even tell him that she is leaving to go north. She is quite willing to hurt Leland in order to leave for Paris with Guy, and she is also willing to abort her child in order to remain "free." One of Cleage's points is that with birth control available, Angel would never have had to make such a choice.

Troubled Women

Though it is important to offer "positive" images of black women, it is also important to recognize the humanity of black women and offer characters who are not perfect, who may have what some might call serious "character flaws." We might still sympathize with them, but they must also take responsibility for their own actions. I see Angel in some ways like Suzan-Lori Parks's Venus (discussed in chapter 4), who may be naive in believing that she will gain riches in England, but is willing to do what she needs to do in order to at least attempt to gain them. Angel's life has been similarly difficult; she has spent her life as a prostitute in one way or another (either literally at Miss Lillie's or figuratively by being the lover of the Italian mobster). She has existed in a world that does not treat black women kindly, and she has responded to that by becoming a survivor. Her survival has required her to become the hard, almost unsympathetic character we meet in *Blues*. She even sings the blues, a musical form that evokes the challenges of life, of life that is full of struggle and sorrow.

Both Angel and Ava Johnson (*Late Bus to Mecca*) are, or have been, prostitutes. Again, the presence of them as characters who are not middle-class protagonists is vitally important. For the contemporary black feminist writer, it is important not only to create images of black women that are "examples" or ideals, but also women who are not the "ideal," who are working-class or poor, who, for one reason or another, exist at the fringes of respectability. Rosa Jenkins, of *Chain,* is another of these characters. Rosa is a sixteen-year-old crack addict who her parents have chained to their apartment's radiator in an attempt to keep her from continuing her crack addiction. These women highlight some of the social and cultural difficulties that also affect black women. By exploring the lives of these women, Cleage addresses some of the challenges that face contemporary black America and contemporary black women.

It is also vitally important that issues such as prostitution and drug addiction are engaged by black feminist playwrights. As we will see, these issues are prominent in the works of Corthron (particularly *Breath, Boom* and *Splash Hatch*) and in the works of Parks (albeit more obliquely). Cleage's plays embrace the complexity of the lives of black women and do not shy away from engaging with "negative" issues or images. When watching *Chain,* we empathize with Rosa's parents and share in their despondency. We might consider what we might do if we were in their circumstances, plagued with a drug-addicted teenager while we try to work full-time in order to survive. We might share in their frustration as they try to find ways to keep Rosa away from her boyfriend and the other bad influences that surround her every day. Rosa's parents, like so many black parents, hoped that their hard work would enable them to give their children a better life; they could not, however, protect her from the violent world around her. How does one begin to fight the plague of drug addiction that afflicts blacks, particularly blacks in inner cities? Cleage does not offer us a solution, but *Chain* challenges us to consider what leads to the person who Rosa might become—mother to a drug-addicted child, perhaps, but likely someone who requires social services and ultimately contributes little or nothing positive to her community or to society. Cleage does not explain how Rosa and her family come to be in these circumstances, but certainly both race and class contribute.

May of *Bourbon at the Border* is likewise troubled. Her trouble stems directly from racist violence. As one of the Freedom Summer volunteers, she and her husband Charlie have been tragically altered by their participation in their struggle for civil rights.[4] The pain of May and Charlie is both physical and spiritual. The violence visited upon them in a Mississippi jail cell has left Charlie physically disabled; he walks with a limp. It has also left him depressed and suffering from post-traumatic stress disorder. He has been hospitalized several times for attempting suicide, but he has never turned that violence against anyone but himself. May, who was beaten and raped in jail, suffers from the emotional toll that rape takes on a woman; she also suffers from the pain of having to watch her husband fight demons that she cannot banish for him.

Complicated characters, though, are appealing to audiences. In some ways, the women of these later plays are more complex than the women of *Flyin' West*. Cleage cites it as one of her goals to create "interesting, complicated, black women characters" (Bashir 19). The ways in which these characters resonate with us as an audience are complex, and their complexity resonates with a reality for us. These women confront the issues that face them, whether the issue is drugs, the aftereffects of rape, or trying to live life in poverty. It is so vitally important that these representations, in their complexity, generate representations of black women that are different than the stereotyped images that have populated theatre and film.

Drawing (on) History

The histories upon which Cleage draws the materials for her plays vary, but in all of them, they expose her audience to something about which they may not be very familiar. Cleage commented that "One of the things I like is a theatre full of black folks! We all laugh at the same stuff. We all cry at the same stuff. We are a community that shares a history and there's a real sweetness when we come together like that" (Bashir 18). This is particularly true of *Flyin' West* and *Bourbon at the Border*. These plays bring history into the present (quite literally so in *Bourbon*) and demonstrate that the issues of concern to black feminists have been consistent through time.

The bits and pieces of history, like the "scraps of memories" in Julie Dash's film *Daughters of the Dust*, are reminders of the complex history of African Americans. In *Flyin' West*, Will talks about being taken in by Seminole Indians when he escaped from the plantation. There was a history of African Americans working with Native Americans, being sheltered by them after escaping from slavery, and even fighting with them against whites in several rebellions. The story of the "Exodusters" themselves is also an overlooked segment of history; it is not generally known by the average African American unless she or he has made a concerted effort to find out specifics about history.

Cleage engages many issues and facts from the Harlem Renaissance period in *Blues*. While Josephine Baker and Langston Hughes are very recognizable, Bruce Nugent is not. The history of the Cotton Club and other clubs that were primarily entertainment for whites, and run by whites, is sometimes overlooked because of the support and fame garnered by so many of the black artists who performed at the Cotton Club. Cleage's inclusion of Guy and her deliberate references to a gay community in Harlem during the Renaissance reflects the developments in historical and cultural studies unearthing gay and lesbian history. She also offers us a glimpse of what Depression-era Harlem was going to become: a place of high unemployment, dreams that slip away, and life in poverty. Leland represents part of the Great Migration, the large migration of blacks from the rural South to the urban North in search of jobs and opportunity, and an escape from racist violence. In some way, the murder of Sam heralds the end of Harlem's golden age.

By engaging with Freedom Summer in *Bourbon at the Border,* Cleage specifically brings the past (specifically the civil rights era) into the present (Detroit in 1995). By centering her play on the aftereffects of racist violence on May and Charlie, Cleage connects some of the problems of contemporary black America to the 1960s. Charlie's severe, suicidal depression is rooted in events that happened some thirty years before the time of the play. The effects of racism physically travel with him through time, carried in his body. Similarly, for May, the aching memory of rape never leaves her consciousness, nor does the pain suffered by her husband. Cleage also offers us a view back on May and Charlie as workers that summer in Mississippi, making their past (and our past as a nation) explicit.

The use of history, explicitly feminist issues, and the ways in which Cleage continually meshes the issues of race, gender, and sexuality make her one of the most feminist playwrights of the last fifteen years.

3 We Are the Daughters of Aunt Jemima: Remembering Black Women's History

In the contemporary world, when representations of African Americans are at issue, there are few noted exceptions to the "minstrelsy" of Hollywood and mainstream theatre. It remains difficult to find revolutionary mimetic content in the majority of the dramatic arts. There are plays that are informed by an understanding of black history in the United States during the nineteenth and twentieth centuries and that call upon us not only to remember that history (both its good and bad aspects) but also to carry that history with us into the future. Despite this, the most visible representations of black Americans continue to be funded by Hollywood, which dissembles that its content is radical while reinscribing the racist material that has been part of Hollywood's standard throughout the twentieth century.

Re/Membering Aunt Jemima: A Menstrual Show, by Breena Clarke and Glenda Dickerson, is a refreshingly black feminist examination of the lives of black women and their sometimes dramatic difference from the stereotypes or icons that proliferate within American popular culture. *Re/Membering Aunt Jemima* takes the structure of the old blackface minstrel shows and transforms the idea of the minstrel show into something that attempts to unpack the stereotypes of black women. Its focus on the various constructions of black womanhood and the women who defied those constructions resists the old racist stereotypes.

This is not a "new millennium minstrel show," in the tradition of Spike Lee's *Bamboozled* (2000); Lee's film questions the continued uncritical use of the blackface minstrel characters in contemporary film and television. This show is a *menstrual* show as well as a minstrel show; unlike the traditional minstrel show, this play is primarily about women. It is also a renewal, a sloughing-off of the old to make way for the new.

At the beginning, the company stands in a semicircle, like in the old minstrel shows, with "La Madama Interlock-it-togetherer." She is the interlocutor; in traditional nineteenth-century minstrel shows, the interlocutor was the primary performer. He (for there were rarely women in minstrel shows, and they were never the interlocutor) was usually identified by his prolific use of malapropisms. Unlike the traditional interlocutor, La Madama uses big words properly; she is obviously intelligent. For example, in the introduction, La Madama chastises two of the "menstruals," who begin arguing with and insulting each other, with the following: "Mistresses, I will not put up with this ingenious vituperation by proxy" (35). La Madama is accompanied by several "menstruals," who function as a chorus and who also perform the lines of Aunt Jemima's daughters. The final character is Aunt Jemima herself. The "bo akutia" mentioned in the opening scene is also important; bo akutia is a custom that the Ashanti practiced. It is the "ingenius vituperation by proxy" that La Madama invokes after the first song (35). The process by which one performed bo akutia is as follows: "a person brought a friend to the home of a chief or some other official who had offended him but of whom he was afraid. In the presence of this personage the aggrieved individual pretended to have an altercation with his friend whom he verbally assailed and abused freely. Once he had relieved himself of his pent-up feelings in the hearing of the person against whom they were really intended, the brief ritual ended with no overt acknowledgment by any of the parties involved of what had actually taken place" (Moss). The play itself performs a kind of bo akutia of the minstrel show itself and of the society that created the stereotypes the play seeks to deconstruct. Through this play, Clarke and Dickerson engage with issues of black women's health, representations of the mammy and tragic mulatta, and the history of black women's activism, and ultimately create a genealogy of black womanhood in the United States. Jemima has many children, from several different fathers. Each of the fathers creates a particular type of child. The first four daughters, who comprise the tragic mulatta icon, are the daughters of Colonel Higbee, the white slave master. Later, Jemima becomes involved with Two-Ton, a slave who can pick two tons of cotton a day, and has three more daughters who, like their father, carry heavy burdens. These three daughters represent the strength of black women in the late nineteenth and early twentieth centuries, who blazed paths in religion, education, and women's rights. The third group of sisters' father is Karo, from Dominica; like the first set, they are a mixture of real and fictional women. During the War Between the States, Aunt Jemima and Uncle Ben stay on the plantation while everyone else is off fighting, and they have two daughters who stand up for themselves in spite of tradition.

Fig. 3. Images of Aunt Jemima, from 1927 and 1954, from the author's collection. Courtesy of the author.

Freeing Aunt Jemima from the Pancake Box

La Madama, the interlocutor, is an aspect of Aunt Jemima. As Clarke and Dickerson noted in their essay "Rescuing the Secret Voice," "In the tradition of Santeria, she is called La Madama, the orisa who fearlessly guards the peace of our homes as she presides over our bread baking and clothes making. Aunt Jemima is not a joke to us. On the contrary, we wish to show that African people used to revere the qualities for which she is now denigrated" (85). When the icon is deconstructed, the "re/membered" woman is the strong, enduring woman transported from Africa who enabled her children to survive. Aunt Jemima is an icon long overdue for a critical and artistic unpacking. The figure of the slave "aunt," who took care of slave children on the plantation, has been lost to us. She has been replaced by the figure of a large black woman on a box of pancake mix or a bottle of syrup. The image that has remained is often interchangeable with the "mammy" icon, the large, asexual, maternal house slave who was completely devoted to the master. Granted, the image of Aunt Jemima has changed over the years, but she still exists as an icon. The black woman who invents a successful product (for example, pancake mix) but refuses to be compensated for it appears elsewhere in popular culture; specifically, it is used in the 1934 film version of *Imitation of Life,* where Louise Beavers plays "Aunt Delilah," who creates a pancake mix that makes the family fortune. The choice of Aunt Jemima asks the audience to consider this icon carefully. From where does it come? How does it affect us? What can be gained by closely examining not only the myth of Aunt Jemima but also the sometimes lost history of black women?

Clarke and Dickerson's Aunt Jemima is not simply a revisionist account; rather, the combination of the minstrel show format and the use of the "menstruals" as Jemima's many daughters makes this play an exploration of black womanhood in the United States. Jemima, as a character, undergoes a transformation just as the image of Aunt Jemima was transformed over time (Figure 3). This transformation through time has two aspects. First, Jemima changes from a woman who is unaffected by the beauty dictates of white culture, and who thinks of herself as beautiful, to a woman deeply scarred by that culture. Second, Jemima moves from her comfortable naïveté to realize herself as a savvy, critical agent.

Jemima herself is oblivious both to the myths she perpetuates and to the subtle resistance she provides to the myths. For example, while her daughter Pecola believes that Jemima is ugly because of her "big lips" and nappy hair, Jemima responds, "What's de mattah wid you. Fore we come across de water, everybody look lak me. I ain't ugly. You just thinks I is" (37). When the daughters insist that she is ugly, she maintains, "Ain't got nothing to be ashamed 'bout. I got pretty black skin, I got a beautiful, long neck, I got a fine, rounded shape. I got plenty to smile about" (37). Obviously, Jemima is not plagued by her African features and shape. Her recognition of her own beauty is an act of resistance against the imposition of white standards of beauty on black women.

Though she does not give in to self-hate, she is not the agitator for change, at least not early in the play, that some of her daughters are. At the Chicago World's Fair, while Aunt Jemima introduces her pancake mix through the Davis Milling Company, daughters Anna and Bondswoman are in the next tent, "lifting as they climb" (39). Jemima resists their feminism and race consciousness before she recognizes them as her own daughters. Her lack of political consciousness in the face of racism and sexism is evident, "When the politically incorrect, internationally acclaimed Aunt Jemima diversified, she made so much money that she bought herself a full-length mink coat and hired herself a chauffeur to drive her around in her Cadillac convertible" (40). Even this "political incorrectness" does not simply stand; as she attends the Miss America pageant, where her daughter Dysmorphia has won, she chastises, "In the country that's just how they buys cows. Ah don't see why ya'll don't just bring in the auction block and sell 'em all together" (41). She likens the beauty pageant to the slave auction block and the selling of livestock, certainly a feminist position.

The re-membering of Aunt Jemima could not be complete without a reference to Hattie McDaniel and her Oscar-winning performance in *Gone With the Wind*. As mammy and Aunt Jemima are interchangeable, so are McDaniel and mammy in the eyes of the culture at large. McDaniel has long been regarded as the epitome of political incorrectness and has been blamed for embodying a stereotype in a way that facilitated the stereotype's transformation into a media icon. Before *Gone With the Wind* had even opened, Walter White and the NAACP publicly threatened, and then carried out, a large-scale campaign against black actors who performed stereotyped roles; McDaniel was one of their targets. However, McDaniel honestly believed that Hollywood would change after awarding her an Oscar, and by the presence of black actors who would take and attempt to transform stereotyped roles, as she believed she did with Mammy.[1] McDaniel was, after all, very successful in Hollywood and achieved a kind of "American Dream" from her film and television work. Clarke and Dickerson invoke her as follows:

LA MADAMA: Aunt Jemima, America's Grand Mammy, remained true to fact and tradition. Tinsel Town beckoned.

MENSTRUAL: Beating out a score of imitators, Aunt Jemima won the coveted role of the faithful colored retainer in an epic motion picture of the old South.

MENSTRUAL: And the winner for Best Actress in a supporting role is: Aunt Jemima.

AUNT JEMIMA: Thank you, friends, colleagues, and members of the Academy. Ah hope that my winning this award will be an inspiration to the youth of my race, that it will encourage them to aim high and work hard, and take the bitter with the sweet. Ah did my best and God did the rest (41).

Later, in response to her daughter Bondswoman's urging her to not be complicit in her own oppression, Jemima responds, "Why should I complain about making $7000 a week playing a mammy. If I didn't I'd be making $7 a week actually being one," another quote attributed to McDaniel (44).[2] She knew whereof she spoke; in 1931, McDaniel herself was working as a maid in Hollywood, waiting for her break. McDaniel embodies the reasons we wrestle with images like mammy and Aunt Jemima. On the one hand, one can condemn her for her naïveté, believing that roles for blacks might be transformed in the 1930s and 1940s. On the other hand, McDaniel did not abandon or divorce herself from her blackness or blacks in general. During World War II, she entertained black soldiers for the USO; she fought against restrictive covenants designed to keep blacks from buying homes in white neighborhoods. While Walter White's campaign against her made it difficult for her to work, her creation of the role of Beulah on *The Beulah Show* radio program opened up opportunities for blacks to perform in roles that were not supporting roles to whites. When the show moved to television, McDaniel again played Beulah, offering a television show about blacks that did not use stereotypical dialect.

Jemima does not remain naive; she grows and changes with her daughters, and suffers more as time goes on. She becomes weary of carrying not only the burden of black womanhood, but also the burden of the stereotypes that have plagued black women for centuries.

Demythologizing the Tragic Mulatta

While still on the plantation, Aunt Jemima has daughters by several different men. This is both historically accurate and a comment on contemporary black women who may have children by several different fathers. In the historical context, slave women had children by their masters and whomever their master assigned them to "marry." Whether or not these were love matches is up for debate, and is also dependent upon the particular situation. The daughters that she has by Colonel Higbee form different aspects of the icon of the tragic mulatta.

As I examined in depth in *Mammies No More,* the "tragic mulatta" has had multiple incarnations in literature from the eighteenth through the twentieth centuries. There was also a distinct difference between the ways she was represented by whites and by blacks. Both of these are elements of the tragic mulattas who are the daughters of Aunt Jemima. The white representation of the mulatta is of a woman who is nearly white by virtue of her parentage; she looks white and can pass as white. Her whiteness gives her access to the refinement that is part of whiteness, but her nearly invisible blackness plagues her life until she is destroyed. Usually, she dies by her own hand; she cannot be permitted to "infiltrate" whiteness and white culture, and she is not "really black." She does not fit anywhere.

For black writers, however, there is a good deal more sympathy for the light-skinned black woman, as long as she maintains her identity as black and works for the community. Part of her "tragedy" is that she represents the rape of her mother by a white man. If she abandons her community by passing for white, then she is likely to come to disaster.

Dorothy, the first child, is based on the real woman Dorothy Dandridge, a black actress of the 1940s and 1950s. Dorothy has some understanding of the place that she occupies by virtue of her parentage:

> My old Man was a white old man
> My old Mammy's black
> Wonder what I'm gonna do
> Being neither white nor black.
> I got the blues.
> The tragic mulatta blues! (36)

Dandridge's "tragic mulatta blues" were twofold. First, as a lighter-skinned black woman, she was typically cast in "tragic" (dramatically melodramatic) roles, like her role in the film *Carmen Jones.* She was, in fact, biracial. Recent interest in Dandridge has been spurred by both the HBO film *Introducing Dorothy Dandridge* and by Donald Bogle's much anticipated biography. In real life, Dandridge was a tragic figure; she was viewed as a black Marilyn Monroe, because both of them were cast in sexual roles, and both committed suicide. A series of failed marriages, numerous unsatisfying affairs, and a career that drew controversy for the roles that she played, all contributed to her suicide. Despite the perception of Dandridge as unintelligent and politically unaware, she developed a keen insight for the predicament in which she found herself. While she resisted the stereotype of the tragic mulatta that had developed in literature and film, she also understood that, unwittingly, she lived in that space:

What was I? That outdated "tragic mulatto" of earlier fiction? Oddly enough, there remains some validity in this concept, in a society not yet integrated. I wasn't fully accepted in either world, black or white. I was too light to satisfy Negroes, not light enough to secure the screen work, the roles, the marriage status available to a white woman. [. . .] Whites weren't quite ready for full acceptance even of me, purportedly beautiful, passable, acceptable, talented, called by the critics every superlative in the lexicon employed for a talented and beautiful woman. Yet the barrier was there. (Dandridge 154–55)

The choice of Dandridge, who embodied the tragic mulatta both in film and in life, emphasizes several things. First, stereotypes develop from perceptions of real lives. Though these may be isolated, they come to represent the "norm" even while they are very specific. Second, it is not always easy to subvert or escape the roles in which you are cast. Dandridge was aware of the political ramifications of the roles she played, yet she (like many others) loved acting and performing, and hoped that her presence would open doors for others. She was nominated for an Oscar for her role in *Carmen Jones;* even Otto Preminger, who directed the film, told her the United States was not ready for a black leading lady, no matter how light-skinned. She commented that, "There was a limit to the professional vehicles available to me, as there was a limit to my acceptance in the white world and to white men. Whore roles were there, of course, like Bess in *Porgy and Bess,* or Carmen Jones. America was not geared to make me into a Liz Taylor, a Monroe, a Gardner. My sex symbolism was as a wanton, a prostitute, not as a woman seeking love and a husband, the same as other women" (183). She realized, perhaps too late, that the life-role in which she had been cast was inescapable. The other three children fathered by Colonel Higbee are:

Marie, child born with a rattlesnake in her hand,
  Pecola, a little red baby who cried melodramatically all the time,
  And Dysmorfia, who was half black and half white, but the black skin didn't show as long as she kept her clothes on. (Clarke and Dickerson 36)

Marie is Marie Leveau, the "Voodoo Queen of New Orleans." Marie is as much mythical character as she was real. The "real" Marie lived in New Orleans in the nineteenth century. Though the date of her birth is fuzzy, to say the least, her first marriage was recorded as 1819, and her death was in 1881. Much information on Marie derives from books of stories and myths of New Orleans and New Orleans "Voodoo"; they are unfortunately tainted by white misunderstandings of voudoun practices. The most interesting and illuminating treatment of Marie's life is Jewel Parker Rhodes's first novel, *Voodoo Dreams.* As in other of her novels, Rhodes evokes the historical period and persons while creating their narratives.

Marie was, at least in myth, a light-skinned black woman (probably a mixture of black, Native American, and white); she was free, not a slave, yet had access to white society. Most blacks came into contact with white society as slaves, and because Marie was not a slave, this should have limited her contact with New Orleans whites. As the "Voodoo Queen of New Orleans," Marie had uncharacteristic power over people in various communities in New Orleans. As a myth, she is a larger-than-life powerful black woman. Unlike the "tragic" mulatta, Leveau maintained some control over her life, and she was not the unhappy figure that Dandridge was. Clarke and Dickerson complicate the stereotype by revealing that the stereotype does not hold true to all light-skinned black women.

Pecola may be recognizable as the name of the subject of Toni Morrison's novel *The Bluest Eye*. As a literary creation whose existence was imagined from the lives and experiences of young black girls living in a racist society, Pecola wanted to be white more than anything. Morrison's moving novel describes the effects of racism on black children, especially young girls. Pecola endures social ostracism, incest, and madness throughout the story. Morrison's character is not the only character upon which Clarke and Dickerson's character is based. Pecola may be more recognizable as "Aunt Delilah's" daughter "Peola" from the 1934 film *Imitation of Life*. Peola was played by another real-life "tragic mulatta," Fredi Washington. Washington worked little in Hollywood, because her very light skin that enabled her to pass as white restricted her to playing mulatta roles. She was too light to be cast opposite black actors in black Hollywood films, and because she was black she could not be cast in white roles; in either case, the apparent result on the screen was an interracial relationship. Both Peola and Pecola desire whiteness because of the advantages that come with whiteness, ones that they can clearly see. Both characters embody the psychic and emotional damage caused by racism and racist standards of beauty. Neither Pecola nor Peola ultimately succeeds in her desire for whiteness; Pecola becomes a shadow of herself after years of abuse, and Peola's excursion into the world of passing is the act that breaks her mother's heart (Delilah dies of a broken heart, and Peola leaves her world to return for her mother's funeral). Clarke and Dickerson's Pecola says little, but notably near the end of the play, she says to Aunt Jemima, "Mama, if you pass me on the street. You mustn't see me. Or own me. Or claim me," echoing Peola's cautionary words to Aunt Delilah in *Imitation of Life*.

Dysmorfia is also a creation. Characters like her first appear in the nineteenth-century blackface minstrel shows as the daughter of "Old Zip Coon." Dysmorphia, according to the Oxford English Dictionary, is "Malformation or deformity, esp. as a congenital condition of the face or head."

Body dysmorphic disorder is a condition in which someone believes there is something wrong with some part of their body. They become so sensitive to their perceived difference that they isolate themselves from others. "The word *dysmorphia* on its own usually indicates a genetic condition in which a part of the body has grown out of proportion" (Quinion). Dysmorfia, therefore, believes that her blackness is the "congenital deformity" with which she has been born. After all, her blackness is something that she believes she has to hide. Her perception of her lips as too big is also part of her "disorder"; she sees them as a deformity that has to be hidden. Also, when she hides her blackness, she is, for all intents and purposes, white. She covers her face with cornstarch "in case de black creep out from underneath my clothes" (37). Her successful efforts to hide her blackness allow her to win the Miss America pageant; only a black woman who passed for white, or who could pass for white, could win the Miss America pageant. The reference here to Vanessa Williams, the first black woman to win the Miss America pageant in 1984, is obvious; Williams's reign as Miss America was cut short by the publication of nude photos of her in *Penthouse* magazine. Williams's blackness and the idea of the sexually promiscuous black woman merged to re-create Williams in the mold of the tragic mulatta. Each of Jemima's four tragic mulatta daughters reveals different aspects of the lives of light-skinned black women, deconstructing the notion of a uniform identity.

Black Women's Health Issues

Clarke and Dickerson also examine many of the health issues that face black women through their choice of characters, and through Aunt Jemima's own health. These issues include reproductive rights, cancer, and female circumcision.

Susie-Faye, president of the "Planned Parenthood ConFederatation of America," is one of the children of Karo, a "smooth brown man of mystery" who hailed from "Dominica" (38). Karo's syrup is a perfect match for Jemima's pancakes, and Karo's daughters defy expectations of them. Faye Wattleton was the first black woman to become the president of Planned Parenthood. As the first black woman to head Planned Parenthood, Wattleton defied years of tradition in that organization, which had not had a woman or a practitioner (Wattleton is a nurse-midwife) as president in decades, and it had never had a nonwhite president. Wattleton's experience as a nurse-midwife led her to fight actively for women's autonomy in issues surrounding childbearing; she saw the difficulties women encountered with efforts to control their fertility. Her choice to become a member of

Planned Parenthood, however, had her join an organization that had ties to eugenics and had actively pursued the sterilization of poor women and women of color. In spite of this dubious association, Wattleton believes that choice—in birth control and abortion—is that of the woman who must live her own life in accordance to her own beliefs. In addition, women's freedom is only complete if she has freedom over her own body: "My training and experience as a nurse and nurse-midwife were invaluable in teaching me, as Margaret Sanger's profession taught her, that a woman's health and her right to control reproduction are inextricably linked to her ability to achieve equality" (Wattleton 469). Wattleton's position was in opposition to that of black nationalists and religious leaders who are opposed to abortion in particular. Wattleton's victory was vitally important for an organization that had not been headed by a woman in decades, not only because of her gender but also because of her race. As someone sensitive to issues of forced sterilization and unavailable services for pregnant women and infants, she was able to steer the organization through the Reagan era's attacks on reproductive choice. As Wattleton believes, and as Clarke and Dickerson invoke by their inclusion of her, issues of reproductive rights are vital to black women.

During the War between the States, Aunt Jemima and Uncle Ben stay on the plantation while everyone else is off fighting, and they have two daughters, one of whom is "Aminata, a headstrong girl full of determination" (38). Aminata is the play's first reference to an African woman, a tribute to the widening interest of black feminists to issues affecting women of the African diaspora outside U.S. borders. Aminata Diop, a woman from Mali, refused to be subjected to the practice of "female circumcision." The issue of circumcision/clitoridectomy is an important one in the script, and the characters refer to it several times. It is obviously a serious issue for African women, and one that remains contentious. The first reference is to Aminata herself. As reported in the *Nocirc Newsletter* in 1992, "After she was beaten by her father for refusing to be circumcised, Aminata Diop, 23, fled from Mali, Africa, to France. Her request for asylum was denied by the French government because the Charter of Geneva has no provision covering people seeking protection for gender-related circumstances; however, she will be allowed to stay in France, where female circumcision has been outlawed" (3). In the play, Aunt Jemima is concerned that her daughter will be subjected to such a procedure:

> MENSTRUAL: Uncle Ben say she got to have a clitoridectomy before she gets married.
> AUNT JEMIMA: Oh, lord, has she got the nervousness?

MENSTRUALS: No!

AUNT JEMIMA: Has she got the catalepsy?

MENSTRUALS: No!

AUNT JEMIMA: She been hysterical?

MENSTRUALS: No!

AUNT JEMIMA: Oh, lord, don't tell me my chile's been masturbatin'! (*falls over in a dead faint*) (42).

While comic, this scene emphasizes the perspective that clitoridectomy is not a necessary surgery, while it also documents the reasons why women over the centuries have been subjected to such surgery. Many forms of clitoridectomy have serious effects on the health of women; there are risks of infection, and the most invasive procedures make intercourse and childbirth painful, complicated procedures.

Jemima's daughters are not the only ones who struggle with health issues. As their mother, and as the representation of the burdens of black women, Jemima suffers from a series of debilitating conditions. Clarke and Dickerson tap into the list of diseases that disproportionately affect black women: breast cancer, debilitating fibroid tumors, and diabetes. Jemima endures a mastectomy, a hysterectomy, and the amputations of her feet. This element is almost hidden within the text, but it is very significant. These conditions are all realities in the lives of black women in the United States, who statistically receive poorer health care and often do not receive medical intervention until the most radical procedures are necessary to save their lives.

Aunt Jemima's amputations require her to go and live on the pancake box. Near the end of the play, Clarke and Dickerson invoke another, contemporary black woman as Jemima. This time, it is the most heartfelt example of the lives of black women in the contemporary United States: the case of Eleanor Bumpers. Bumpers's case has been used by critical race feminists in their assessment of black women's legal situations in the United States. A menstrual relates:

MENSTRUAL: She was sixty-six years old and weighed three hundred pounds. She had arthritis, high blood pressure, and diabetes. The cops said she shouted that she would kill anybody who tried to evict her (44).

Bumpers was being evicted from her Bronx apartment for being five months behind on her rent; she owed less than $500. Though the police were supposed to treat her as mentally ill, they entered the apartment in full SWAT gear, shot off her hand when she wielded a knife, and then fired a shotgun aimed at her chest, killing her. None of the officers were injured.

Moments from the Bumpers case are interspersed with a song, sung by Jemima, that also recounts her physical condition:

> It's a goddamn shame
> What they do to me
> What will it take
> To set me free?
> Goddamn, goddamn!

Clarke and Dickerson's song recalls Nina Simone's song, "Mississippi Goddamn," that recounted the struggles of the Civil Rights Movement. The illnesses suffered by Jemima have caused her to be confined to the pancake box; the illnesses suffered disproportionately by black women are hurdles to the survival of black women.

> Don't read my pap smear
> For a year
> They finally tell me
> I'm filled with fear
> Cancer's eating up my womb
> Mother Earth, you'll be my tomb

Black women die at much higher rates than white women from cancers, particularly breast cancer, uterine cancer, and ovarian cancer. "African-American women have lower incidence rates of the disease, but have higher mortality rates. Moreover, African-American women present at a younger age and with more aggressive disease. As research has shown, not having had a screening mammogram for one to three years prior to diagnosis was associated with 52 percent of late-stage breast cancer cases. The authors [of a research study published in the *Journal of the National Cancer Institute*] state that to improve breast cancer outcomes, priority should be placed on reaching unscreened women and encouraging them to have mammograms—especially older, unmarried, less educated, and/or low income women, whom they found were less likely to have been screened" (NIH news press release 2004). While black women are less likely to contract or die from uterine cancer, "the African American mortality rate [from cervical cancer] continues to be more than double that of Whites" (National Cancer Institute 2005). Aunt Jemima laments the state of her health:

> What they do to me, Goddamn
> Hysterectomy, goddamn
> What they do to me, goddamn
> Clitoridectomy, goddamn

What they do to me, Goddamn
Mastectomy, goddamn
Cancer wrecked me, goddamn
Cancer wrecked me, goddamn (44)

The trials and tribulations of Jemima and her daughters have the ultimate effect of making her an activist in the model of her activist children.

Ain't Ah a Woman?

The history of black women's activism forms the center of Clarke and Dickerson's play. They intersperse real women with stereotypes, television characters, and composite characters in order to capture the breadth of black women's activism in the United States. The primary daughters who are the activists are the children of Two-Ton, but ultimately, the majority of her daughters become activists in some way.

Jemima's second mate is Two-Ton, a slave so-named because "he could pick two ton of cotton any day of the week." She has three children with Two-Ton; these children are distinguished by their efforts to improve the lives of others; they are the "little hammers" left to her after Two-Ton dies with a hammer in his hand.[3] The explicit linking of the John Henry legend with the character Two-Ton brings additional emphasis on the nature and power of that place where life and legend mix and become myth.

Like their father, who could bear the weight of two tons of cotton, the daughters of Two-Ton bear the weight of bettering the world. These three characters are all based on historical women; there are no stereotypes or myths here. They were all nineteenth-century activists, concerned with women's rights and civil rights. Anna Julia is Anna Julia Cooper, whose *A Voice from the South* established her as one of the leading black thinkers of the late nineteenth and early twentieth centuries. Her presence in the play reinforces its feminist roots. Cooper, a writer and educator, emphasized not only the importance of education to blacks in general, but also advocated for the importance of black women in the struggle for full emancipation. The inclusion of Cooper brings an early black feminist presence to the history of feminism; Cooper's 1897 critique of the racism of white women and the sexism of black men anticipates the development of black feminism formally in the 1960s and 1970s.

Like many of her white contemporaries, Cooper believed in the moral superiority of women, and viewed it as a duty or responsibility for women to reform society. The club motto "lift as we climb" is attributed to her, demonstrating her view that it was also imperative for those with education and privilege (the black middle class) to help the community by giving back to it. She also recognized that the freedom of black women was a priority, and that the other civil rights struggles were less than complete. In *A Voice from the South*, she wrote: "The colored woman of to-day occupies, one may say, a unique position in this country. . . . She is confronted by both a woman question and a race problem, and is as yet an unknown or an unacknowledged factor in both" (45).

Rebecca, called to preach, is Mother Rebecca Jackson, a black woman elder in the Shaker tradition who led an urban community of Shakers in Philadelphia. Although black women who preached were not a complete rarity in the nineteenth century, they were not common. Until the entrance of Jackson into the spiritual community, the Shakers were almost exclusively white, living in private spiritual communities located in rural New York and New England.

Jackson's success within the predominantly white Shaker community, and her insistence on creating and maintaining an urban Shaker community are testaments to the support she received from the Shakers and from blacks in Philadelphia. It was not easy for Jackson, often taunted and ostracized among other black faiths and by many black ministers, to assert herself as a woman with "unusual" spiritual beliefs. It was also very difficult for her to live in isolation among the white Shakers in their rural setting, because community was so important to her.

Bondswoman, who fled north, represents one of the more famous nineteenth-century black women, Harriet Tubman. She "followed the North Star and the moss on the trees," first taking herself to freedom and then facilitating the escape of other slaves from the South. (37). Her legendary position as a conductor on the Underground Railroad is well known; like the other characters that are daughters of Two-Ton, Bondswoman's burden is a heavy one, but vitally important for the growth and development of free blacks in the United States.

These three daughters represent the strength of black women in the late nineteenth and early twentieth centuries who blazed paths in religion, education, and women's rights. Their strength differentiates them from their sisters. While they are not the only "strong black women" in the play, their strength lies in their dedication to improving the lives of black men and women in the United States, and not only in their own social or economic benefit. Of the three, it is Anna Julia Cooper who is most present; this is not surprising, because Cooper's extant written texts provide abundant quotes, some recognizable, that detail her beliefs about the issues facing black women at the turn of the twentieth century. Clarke and Dickerson are certain to quote Cooper's most famous passage:

MENSTRUAL (TRUE WOMAN³): Only the black woman can say "when and where I enter, in the quiet, undisputed dignity of my womanhood, without violence and without suing or special patronage, then and there the whole Negro race enters with me" (39).

Clarke and Dickerson cast Cooper as a "true woman," and a "proponent of the tenets of the cult of true womanhood," which may not be entirely accurate (40). The four "cardinal virtues" of "true womanhood" were piety, purity, submissiveness, and domesticity. However, the nature of Cooper's fight for black women is only partially about the four virtues. The embracing of these "virtues" was important only in the assertion that black women were as feminine as white women; this particular tactic, as it would come to be embraced by the black Club Women of the early twentieth century, was also used by many middle-class blacks. From Du Bois to Angelina Grimké, efforts to show the humanity of blacks sharply contrasted with the continued presence of scientific racism, which considered blacks uneducable and unassimilable into American society.

"Sapphire, a girl who could not be tamed by any man, and the newborn baby, Freedom Fighter" are the daughters who defy the pressure from earlier times to be graceful in their resistance to racism, sexism, and classism. "When Freedom Fighter grew up, she became involved with so many slave revolts and shootouts, she was on the FBI's most wanted list" (38). Freedom Fighter is an amalgamation of Angela Davis, who was on the FBI's most wanted list and was implicated in shootouts (although she never shot a gun), and the other black women who fought for civil rights in the 1950s and 1960s, like Ella Baker and Fannie Lou Hamer. Sapphire is the only fictional daughter of Karo; she began life as a character on the *Amos 'n Andy* television show and become a stereotype of black women.

Angela Davis is a revolutionary black woman who defied racialized and gendered expectations. The textual references to the character Freedom Fighter are vague enough that many other women could be the intended reference. As activists, Davis, Baker, and Hamer were involved with the revolutionary movements of the 1960s, from SNCC to the Black Panthers. Davis's troubles with the U.S. government began when she was fired from her position at the University of California San Diego by then-governor Ronald Reagan because of her association with the Communist Party. She was harassed because of her friendship and advocacy for the Soledad Brothers; she was placed on the most wanted list because she allegedly gave weapons to Jonathan Jackson, brother of George Jackson (one of the Soledad Brothers). He used them to open fire in a Marin County courthouse in the chambers of the judge who had sentenced his brother to prison. Davis ran, was eventually captured, tried, and acquitted of all charges. Her ability to triumph over adversity established her as a model for young black women in the early 1970s.

Though Davis has received much attention from the general public, the work of black women in the South during the Civil Rights Movement, particularly in the tumultuous 1960s, is much less part of popular culture. Ella Baker had long been involved with the NAACP and with SCLC from the 1940s until the 1960s.[4] She organized students at Shaw University in Raleigh, North Carolina, in the spring of 1960; from their sit-ins, SNCC (Student Nonviolent Coordinating Committee) was formed. Through her voting rights work, she helped found the Mississippi Freedom Democratic Party (MFDP). Baker's path crossed that of Fannie Lou Hamer in Mississippi, where Hamer had lived all of her life. Hamer volunteered to go to the courthouse in Montgomery County in an attempt to register to vote. She and the other black volunteers were jailed and beaten; Hamer sustained an eye injury that left her partially blinded. In spite of threats against her life, Hamer went on to help found the MFDP, and worked for civil rights until her death.

While Freedom Fighter struggles against racial oppression, Sapphire, the fictional creation, first emerged in the 1950s with the television show, *Amos 'n Andy*. As Kingfish's wife, Sapphire is noted for loquaciousness and sassiness. In the tradition of the sisters fathered by Karo, Sapphire is a contested character. Sapphire's resistance is centered on gender; her adversaries tend to be sexist. As a creation of both white and male imagination, however, the character of Sapphire is not seen as powerful, but rather manipulative. Sapphire spars with a black male foil, one whose "lack of integrity, and use of cunning and trickery provides her with an opportunity to emasculate him through her use of verbal put-downs" (Jewell 45). The image of the sapphire, an autonomous, assertive black woman, is like the other two characters who are daughters of Karo; both Freedom Fighter and Suzie-Faye's historical figures are autonomous and assertive black women who can be seen as somewhat "matriarchal." This notion, engendered by the Moynihan Report, maintains that black women are too strong, and that they eclipse the masculinity of black men and claim it as their own. In other words, these three representations emerge out of the historically assertive black woman, who is often seen as defiant by the dominant culture and also by black men because she chooses to take power and assert it. Clarke and Dickerson challenge the notion that strong black women are a negative, rather than positive, force in the community by presenting women whose primary concern is for the race as a whole; they are "race women."

The two daughters of Uncle Ben, Aminata and Anita, begin as more obedient characters, but eventually find that the cost for their obedience was far too high. Both of these daughters are real women; the characters' birth during the Civil War is symbolic of their growing up in a post–civil rights era. In theory, both of them should have the advantages that come as a result of the liberation struggles of the 1960s. Unfortunately, they are both wrong about how far they have come as black women. While Aminata seeks asylum from a clitoridectomy, Anita discovers that sexism will still work in favor of black men against black women.

Anita follows Uncle Tom to "Yarvard Law School"; Anita has an opportunity that the women who came before her have not had. The next time Jemima sees her is at the confirmation hearings for Uncle Tom. Clarke and Dickerson save their most ingenious vituperation by proxy for the Clarence Thomas confirmation hearings, and reinforce the feelings of black women (many of them feminists) throughout the United States who were horrified by the proceedings.[5] When Anita challenges Uncle Tom's confirmation, he "has no trouble slipping into America's most beloved minstrel role," that of an Uncle Tom. Jemima assesses the proceedings by declaring, "She got trashed and he got confirmed! Simple as that. Umph!" (44). Like Aminata, Anita refuses to accede to sexist practices in favor of black men. Like the black feminism that Anita Hill did not engage in the Thomas hearings, Anita and Aminata become acutely aware of the effects of sexism and racism on them.

Like Anita and Aminata, Tiny Desiree also finds that the progress she believed had occurred with the Civil Rights Movement and the feminist movement has not yet arrived. Jemima's last child grows from a watermelon seed. Obviously, the association of black people with watermelons emerges with the minstrel show; in addition, the idea of a black child who "jus' growed" recalls Harriet Beecher Stowe's *Uncle Tom's Cabin* and the wild child Topsy. Tiny Desiree (named for Desiree Washington, the Miss Black America contestant raped by boxer Mike Tyson) tells Jemima that she is "gettin' too old to sit up on that box," and argues with Sapphire (43). She claims that she is the "Anita-thisis of Sapphire," in other words, she is unlike Sapphire—she is not able to "handle" men but, like Anita, discovers the limitations of her gender at the end of the twentieth century.

Inscribed in History

Obviously, Clarke and Dickerson have included a variety of women, both historical and fictional, to populate their play. The importance of these characters lies both in their histories and in their relationships to the stereotypes—particularly the Aunt Jemima/mammy stereotype.

For all its comedy, the root of this variety show parody of the minstrel show is a celebration of black womanhood. Particularly important are the characters who have spent much of their history in obscurity, like Anna Julia Cooper, Marie Leveau, and Rebecca Jackson. Although their presence in the play may not reveal all of their importance, it does at least encourage the curious to discover more about them. Dickerson and Clarke are also able to incorporate stereotypes other than Aunt Jemima, and transform them as well: Pecola and Sapphire appear here because they are as ready for recontextualization as Jemima herself. These characters and historical women remain very public and mediated contestations of black womanhood—with multiple interpretations and values from both black and nonblack communities. Clarke and Dickerson give us a genealogy of black women, both real and imagined, through the history of the United States.

The characters also reflect the progress of black women in the United States through time. Those children born earliest have the most difficulty separating themselves from racist depictions and in asserting a black feminist perspective, one that struggles against all oppressions. These women exist primarily in a nineteenth-century context. In other words, their access to elements of rights based both on gender and race is restricted. The children born last are plagued by the same issues that plague contemporary black women; they struggle with feminism and feminist ideals as they realize, in very painful ways, that their oppression *as black women* does not disappear with advances in civil rights. Their difficulty comes not from attempting to assert a black feminist perspective, but from the necessary task of rescuing it from its vilification.

Recent and contemporary contexts commingle with historical ones. The authors play with the breadth of time they have to work with (nearly three hundred years) and the abundance of incidents and allusions that refer to literary, historical, and cultural references to black women. The rape of the Hoodoo Queen by the roving gang of preppies, and the eleven white male jurors who said that she deserved it, is one example. In the opening of the play, Aunt Jemima is said to have been "discovered covered with feces . . . / And branded with the letters KKK," an obvious reference to the Tawana Brawley case. The authors find ways to stretch, from references to the 1893 World's Fair to Vanessa Williams winning the Miss American contest; in doing so, they also illuminate the point that both racism and sexism still exist, and that black women must continue to fight against these forces; also, by engaging in this black feminist struggle, they are joining with the women who went before them in a similar effort. Finally, Dickerson and Clarke have Aunt Jemima reveal herself with the following monologue:

America who caused the daughters of Africa to commit whoredoms and for-
nications, upon thee be their curse. When they brung me off the ship Ah was
stark naked so's Ah couldn't hide no infirmity. Ah hoed the fields, harvested
the crops, planted córn, carried dried trash, turned manure and worked the
fields. When Ah had my babies, Ah kept on working. Carry they burdens on
my back and work too. Ah been visited by the jumper. Look here what he done.
Ah got stripes over the face, the body and my missing breasts. Though we are
looked upon as things, we sprang from a scientific people. Ah bore thirteen
children. Ain't Ah a woman? (45)

The play reaches back through more than a century to bring this historical
awareness to Clarke and Dickerson's audience, and quotes several important speeches by nineteenth-century black women. This play is filled with
acts of resistance. Even though Aunt Jemima begins the play with a desire
to please her white folks, she becomes radicalized as she ages and through
the influence of many of her daughters. These acts specifically include acts
of resistance against racial, sexual, and class domination. Aunt Jemima, who
begins as the despised stereotype, comes to knowledge and understanding
about black womanhood. She also emerges from the shadows of a reviled
stereotype, a creation of white America, to be revealed as beautiful, strong,
and noble.

4 Battling Images:
Suzan-Lori Parks and Black Iconicity

Suzan-Lori Parks is part of the continuum of African American women play-wrights who have deconstructed and reconstructed the identities and histo-ries of African Americans, particularly those of African American women. Parks's early work examines the relationship of the African American to American society, focusing on racism and its effects on both black women and men. All of Parks's plays use black feminist aesthetics and theory to sculpt statements about African Americans. Her plays engage the questions of identity, history, and representation that are standard to black feminist aesthetics. Parks's method is deconstructive; in other words, she presents images or icons to us and then uncovers their origins, revealing them as problematic.[1] Her more recent plays take on a number of contemporary icons, relating them to the classical "American" figure of Hester Prynne in Nathaniel Hawthorne's *The Scarlet Letter.* Of particular interest to me are her early play, *Death of the Last Black Man in the Whole Entire World,* her pseudo-historical drama *Venus: A Play,* and her recent *In the Blood.* An examination of these three plays reveals the aspects of Parks's feminist aesthetic.

As feminist works, Parks's plays examine negative stereotypes of black women as sexual objects and as the iconic "welfare queen." She also exam-ines the clash between choice and complicity, and how the pressures of living in a racist society create a pathological desire on the part of blacks to erase their blackness. She also demonstrates the importance of black women in the continuation and holding together of black culture.

Black Women as Sexual Objects

One of the issues that has been a consistent subject for black feminist playwrights has been that of the representation of the black woman as sexually promiscuous and perpetually available. These issues of black female sexuality are inextricably connected to views of the black female body as "abnormal" yet enticing because of—or in spite of—its fullness.

Parks addresses all of these issues in *Venus: A Play*. Like Pearl Cleage, Parks works from a historical event; in this case, it is the exhibition, trial, and ultimate dissection and display of Sara Baartman that is the starting place. Unlike Cleage, however, Parks does not remain in either the realm of history or the realm of realism. Parks is concerned with the ways in which the real person, Sara Baartman, became "The Venus Hottentot," an icon for black femininity, the black female body, and black female sexuality.

> THE NEGRO RESURRECTIONIST
> (rest)
> Early in the 19th century a poor wretched woman was exhibited in England under the appellation of the Hottentot Venus. With an intensely ugly figure, distorted beyond all European notions of beauty, she was said to possess precisely the kind of shape which is most admired among her countrymen, the Hottentots.
>
> The year was 1810, three years after the Bill for the Abolition of the Slave-Trade had been passed in Parliament, and among protests and denials, horror and fascination Her show went on. She died in Paris 5 years later: a plaster cast of her corpse was displayed, along with her skeleton, at the Musée de l'Homme. (159)

In reviews of performances of the play, from its initial production at Yale Rep and its subsequent productions in both university and professional theatres, the play is repeatedly characterized as the history of Sara Baartman. A brief investigation into the history of Baartman, who became "The Venus Hottentot," provides us with evidence that, while Parks uses facts from the historical record, her play is not an accurate biography of Baartman. It has confused audience members and critics alike, primarily because though we know that there was a person named "Saartjie Baartman," "The Venus Hottentot," we know little about her life.

In taking "Venus" as the subject of this play, Parks explores the recent interest in Baartman and the ways in which the icon "The Venus Hottentot" has come into contemporary constructions of the black female body. According to Z. S. Strother, "it was the discussions of the constructions of sexuality in science and medicine by Stephen Jay Gould [a 1982 article entitled "The Hottentot Venus"] and Sander Gilman [a 1985 essay in *Critical Inquiry*] that recatapulted her to fame. Since then, Baartman has fast become both an academic and a popular icon for black sexuality and its exploitation" (1). Rather than creating a strict historical account, then,

Parks explores the continuity of black female representation through the icon of Sara Baartman (variously Saartjie, which means "little Sara"), the "Venus Hottentot," in the past and present. I will examine Parks's choice of Baartman as the object/subject of her play, and how, through her playing with history, the text and performance of the play encourages us to reconsider our contemporary readings of black female (and the generally racialized-othered) bodies.

Sara Baartman, a young Khoikhoi (Khosian) woman, was "convinced" to leave South Africa for England, where she imagined she would become rich and be able to return to her homeland. As a Xhosa, she was essentially a slave and would not really have had the option to refuse to leave South Africa. Henrik Caesar exhibited her in England; her exhibition drew a lawsuit by abolitionists, who claimed that she was enslaved. It was determined that she was in England of her own accord. In 1814, Baartman was moved to Paris, where she was exhibited until Parisians lost interest in her. According to Marang Setshwaelo, Baartman was forced into prostitution in order to survive; she died an alcoholic, probably infected with both tuberculosis and syphilis (Setshwaelo). Georges Cuvier, the anatomist, dissected her after her death and is the person initially responsible for her display in the Musee de l'Homme. What killed Sara Baartman is unknown; Cuvier was not interested in an autopsy, only in his "scientific" research on her body. Cuvier's dissection of her was focused on her sexuality. Her genitalia were displayed for several years; her skeletal remains, some preserved organs, and a plaster cast of her body were stored there until efforts on the part of the South African government persuaded the French government that she should be returned. Her remains were repatriated to South Africa in May 2002 and interred in August 2002.

Baartman's body was the means through which she was exploited and also her "claim to fame," as it were. She "suffered [*sic*] from steatopygia, an enlargement of the behind"; she was anomalous particularly in a Western Europe in which the sexualization of female bodies did not include the behind (Strother 1). Alexander Dunlop and Henrik Caesar transported Sara to England; Caesar became her exhibitor. She joined the freak shows that were popular at the time. Z. S. Strother claims, "In fact, Baartman's success lay in her status as a figure of the anti-erotic, which allowed her to cross from the 'freak show' to the pseudo-educational ethnographic show. It was as the figure of the anti-erotic that Baartman was reassuring to a European audience" (2). Early nineteenth-century fashions for women did not accentuate sexuality; modest necklines and dresses that hung from the shoulder, hiding the body's curves, were the fashion. In addition, Baartman's culture practiced ritual lengthening of the labia, creating what became known as the "Hottentot apron." Though she wore a piece of clothing over the lower front of her body, the audience who viewed her knew about this physical "anomaly." There are no photographs of Baartman, so we must rely on drawings and paintings, which are influenced by the artist's perception of her, and the plaster cast made by Georges Cuvier shortly after her death.

The exaggerations of her body by the various artists and naturalists who drew her emphasize just how different Europeans wanted Baartman to be. According to contemporary researchers, she was not as big as pictured; the documentary film *The Life and Times of Sara Baartman* includes footage of both her skeleton and the plaster cast, which reveals the bias of those who drew or painted her. Many drawings of Baartman make her look about twice as big as she was. In life, she was less than five feet tall and weighed a "hefty" ninety-eight pounds. The plaster cast of her body looks rather "normal"; even in contemporary obsession with obesity and body-mass index, Baartman would have had a Body Mass Index (BMI) of 21, within the normal range for someone 4'9". Some drawings depict a woman who appears to weigh more than two hundred pounds. It is in this notion of representing the "everyday" that Baartman came to signify not herself, an individual person who, perhaps, had a larger behind than the average English woman, but rather the black female body and its inherent sexuality. Her strangeness became "familiar," a recognizable sign for the alleged sexual availability of black women. Already exploited in the Americas and in colonial Africa, black women's sexuality was confirmed through the "study" of Baartman.

In embodying the "anti-erotic", then, Baartman did come to iconically signify the black female body and sexuality. As Jan Nederveen Pieterse notes in his 1992 text *White on Black: Images of Africans and Blacks in Western Popular Culture,* "Initially the Hottentot female was regarded as the prototype of the African or black woman. African female sexuality was equated thereafter with female sexuality in general, which in accordance with nineteenth-century medical views was considered 'pathological'" (181). As he notes, the 1893 Italian study, *La Donna Delinquente: la prostitua e la donna normale,* "drew an analogy between the prostitute and the Hottentot woman, both associated with unrestrained sexuality" (181). The enlarged labia of the Khoikhoi were correlated to the labia of prostitutes, particularly those who had long histories of sexually transmitted diseases. Thus, Baartman's sexuality was conflated with that of the prostitute. There was no intimation, according to the aforementioned documentary, of a sexual relationship between Baartman and either Caesar or Dunlop.

Baartman was originally displayed as a "type," but later became almost exclusively an ethnographic or naturalist display, where she was meant to represent the "typical" or "everyday" Khoikhoi woman. Cuvier, the scientist, was not an anatomist, but a naturalist. His efforts in *dissecting* (not performing an autopsy) the body of Sara Baartman were a search for the "missing link" between human and ape, *and* another attempt to prove that Africans were not *human*, but something inferior. This is, in part, the reason why this icon, "Venus Hottentot," for all its inaccuracy and exaggeration, came to represent all women of African descent.

Venus, like Parks's other plays, relies on signs (visual, embodied, and linguistic) of American culture; she engages the codes and manipulates them in order to make her point. As in life, Baartman becomes not herself but rather a figure, "Venus." This is accentuated by the fact that only once during the action of the play is the character referred to as "Saartjie," and never as "Sara." This reference to the character as "Saartjie" happens in Scene 31, the first scene of the play after the overture. (Parks numbers the scenes backward.)[2]

Parks establishes the nature of Venus's attraction in the Overture. Here, one of the chorus members comments:

> An ass to write home about.
> Well worth the admission price.
> A spectacle a debacle a priceless prize, thuh filthy slut.
> Coco candy colored and dressed all in *au naturel*
> She likes when people peek and poke. (7)

Venus is labeled a slut, as someone who likes being looked at and prodded; like all black women, she is always available for sex. It is her behind that is the central element of her attractiveness, and she and the "big butt" become interchangeably sign and signifier. The chain of significations leads from Baartman's steatopygia (and her genitalia) to any large(r) behind.

Her alleged sexual availability becomes the sexual availability of all black women. She was molested in her youth by the character of The Brother, who is the brother of the white man who owns her. It is The Brother's plan to take her to London—or was it her, or some other "hottentot?"

THE BROTHER: Remember me? From way back when?
　About 12 yrs ago?
THE GIRL: Youve growd a beard other than that You havent changed.
THE BROTHER: I wanted you then and I want you now.
　That's partly why we've come here.
　So I can love you properly.
　Not like at home. (23)

Of course, like the other white men who encounter her, he is intrigued by her bottom, gropes her, and then sells her quickly.

The White "Mother" and Exploitation

Parks takes us through Venus's arrival in England, the period of her early display. It is at this point in the play when we encounter the Mother-Showman, another place where Parks diverges significantly from the historical record. Many of the incidents that occur in scenes 27, 25, 24, 20B, 20F, 20H, 20I, and 20J did happen (or at least hold more strictly to the historical record). Sara Baartman was exhibited in London, there was a trial to determine whether or not she was enslaved, and she did tour England. However, her exhibition was run entirely by Henrik Caesar; he did not sell her until after they arrived in Paris. Because no women were actually involved with the exploitation of Sara, Parks must instead be pointing at something else.

The Mother-Showman is played by a woman. Parks instructs that the cast doubling should work so that The Man's Brother, The Mother-Showman, and The Grade-School Chum are all played by the same actor; in the case of the production directed by Richard Foreman, Sandra Shipley played these roles. Parks's creation of a fictional character in the Mother-Showman and her casting instructions for this character negate any attempts to universalize the exploitation of Venus solely on the basis of being female; Venus is exploited because she is both black and female. Mother-Showman believes that Venus will make her wealthy. She has Venus clean up, and presents her as the ninth wonder, the "lowest link in God's Great Chain of Being" (Parks, *Venus* 31). The language of Mother-Showman in the midst of displaying Venus is full of sexual innuendo. For example, in Scene 24, Mother-Showman claims she "Ripped her off thuh mammoth lap of uh mammoth ape! She was uh (*keeping house for him*)" (43). She understands that it is the sexual exploitation of Venus that will earn her the most money. When interest dries up, she kicks Venus (Parks notes that "the act has the feel of professional wrestling but also looks real") (45). It is also a pun, though; Mother-Showman says that the Hottentots have "a whole language of kicks," and they do, in fact, have a language of *clicks*. Her abuse of Venus is opportunistic. She has ten mouths to feed, and having Venus as one of her exhibits brings in enough extra cash to survive. Venus is well aware that she is the largest draw, and requests that she be treated better than the other wonders. Mother-Showman denies her request, and laughs when her "daughter" decides to strike out on her own. Venus needs her protection, Mother-Showman argues:

Don't push me Sweetie.
Next doors a smoky pub
Full of drunken men.
I just may invite them in
One at a time
And let them fuck yr brains out. (56)

When Venus retorts, "They do it anyway," Mother-Showman says, "Well. It's the same for all of us, Love" (57). Venus is aware that it is *not* the same for Mother-Showman as it is for her. As someone who wields power through her race and class (she does essentially run a business), Mother-Showman will never be subject to the same kinds of abuses as Venus, who does not have the advantages of race and class that Mother-Showman has.

By placing Venus's presentation in the hands of a woman, Parks sets us up for a contrast between the exploitation that Mother-Showman, the white woman, enacts and that of The Baron Docteur, the white man. With the Mother-Showman, Venus's sexual exploitation happens indirectly. Mother-Showman's choice to charge a fee for groping (and other sexual favors) places her in the role of a madam, prostituting Venus for cash. Though it is Mother-Showman's responsibility to protect Venus (as she would her own child, we have to wonder), she abuses her power to protect Venus and instead facilitates her sexual exploitation at the hands of other men and at the hands of the Baron, who purchases her from Mother-Showman. She does wonder *why* the Baron wishes to buy her; in fact, she asks three times during their exchange why he wants her. His ultimate response is that he will "get her out of that filthy cage for one. / Teach her French. Who knows" (84).

Venus and her Docteur

The fictionalized love story between Venus and the Baron represents the historical sexual connections between powerful white men and powerless black women. Venus is finally given/sold to The Baron Docteur (who is and is not Cuvier; Cuvier did not have a sexual relationship with Sara), who takes her to Paris and displays her there for other anatomists; he wants to be great ("an anatomical Columbus!"), and Venus is his ticket (124). The Baron's Grade-School Chum confronts him, encouraging him to "dissect her soon, Old Friend." When Grade-School Chum demands that the Baron get rid of her, the Baron claims that he loves her. For Venus, it does not seem like a difficult choice; it appears to her that the Baron is, much like the Man, offering her a choice of a better life than the one she is currently living.

Although he has already paid Mother-Showman for Venus, he addresses himself to her as a suitor (complete with a red heart box of chocolates). Venus asks if he will pay her (which is more than Mother-Showman has done), and he agrees; he agrees to all her demands except for one—her own bedroom.

Their relationship is compelling, for both of them want something very specific out of it. Unfortunately, they do not want the same thing. Venus only wants "love," both emotional and sexual. The Baron can only think about how Venus can make him famous. He recites to her the same ridiculous "love" poem that he sends to his wife; his love for Venus is fabricated as well, but she loves the poem. He masturbates while she eats chocolates; he impregnates her twice (and twice performs abortions on her). When she suggests that he could discover *her* to make himself famous, he is ecstatic.

Venus plays the part of the mistress. Her love for him is also fabricated; she hopes that he will give as much to her as she has to him. In Scene 7, she daydreams that "he will leave that wife for good and we'll get married (we better or I'll make a scene)" (135). As mistress of the house, she will meet Napoleon, have parties, and have servants she can control.[3] Venus sees her relationship with the Baron as something that can give her access to power.

The other "appropriation" of Venus's sexuality takes place in "For the Love of the Venus," which Parks inserts into Venus's story. Scenes from "For the Love of the Venus" are peppered throughout the script and the story of Parks's Venus. In this "play-within-a-play" the Baron and his wife play out their passionless romance; in a "love letter," he writes to her, "My love for you, my love, is artificial / Fabricated much like this epistle" (38–39). The Baron's wife begins to lose her husband to his new infatuation: Africa. The only way for the Baron's wife to regain the attention of her husband is to become that with which he is infatuated: Venus. Distressed that she never sees her husband any more, the Baron's wife disguises herself as the Venus. Thus, Venus's "body" is appropriated by the white woman through an intermediary (her uncle):

> She sez she comes from far uhway where its quite hot.
> She sez shes pure bred Hottentot.
> She sez if Wilds your desire
> She comes from The Wilds and she carries them behind her.
> Wild is her back-ground her fundament so to speak
> And although shes grown accustomed to our civil ways
> She still holds The Wilds within her
> Behind, inside, infront
> Which is to say, that all yr days
> With her will be a lively lovely bliss. (133)

This is the icon of both Venus the character and of black female sexuality; there remains a "wildness," a being-closer-to-nature that becomes a part of the icon of black womanhood.

Venus's difference is exoticized by Mother-Showman, the Baron, and his wife. For each of them, the exotic embodied by Venus has a different significance. For Mother-Showman, Venus's exoticism is to be exploited; it is an avenue to profit, one aspect of power in a capitalist society. The Baron wants to possess the exotic; Venus is his fantasy of sex in abundance and without guilt, all of which is embodied in her body and her blackness. The Baron's wife wants to imitate Venus's exoticism. She attempts to appropriate the colonial object, to imitate the "wildness" of the colonized.

The erotic nature of Venus's large posterior invokes contemporary U.S. popular culture; Sir Mix-A-Lot's 1991 ode to "big butts" ("Baby Got Back") rap music video and the public comments about Jennifer Lopez's behind all reveal or reinforce the ideas that black (and Latina) women have large behinds, and that they are attractive to (primarily, but not exclusively) black men. Despite these positive associations, the negative associations remain. The association of black women with prostitution and ready availability for sex are deeply connected to the Venus Hottentot imagery. The very real facts about Sara's exploitation and the uses to which her particular physiology were put by nineteenth-century "scientists" is a significant part of the codification of racism and colonialism, and the alleged "inherent inferiority" of the African.

Using Hester's Body

While Parks's works tend towards the serious, *The Red Letter Plays* have none of the even vaguely comic or satiric undertones of her earlier works. *In the Blood* is the story of Hester, an illiterate black mother with five children from five different fathers, who is on welfare and struggles to survive with those children. Not unlike Venus, Hester exists as a sexual object to virtually all of those with whom she has contact. Hester's victimization reveals her powerlessness and her objectification even more sharply than Venus's. The adults with whom Hester has contact reveal, both in dialogue with Hester and in confessional soliloquies, the details of their abuses of her.

The sexual objectification of Hester begins with the Doctor, who claims that he is being "forced" to sterilize her. Even though he sees Hester in his sidewalk clinic (complete with advertising sandwich board), he does not take care of her immediate problem; she is having severe stomach pains and has a fever. Instead, he is consumed with the removal of her "womanly parts," attempting to gain her consent for the surgery (43). In his confession, he reveals that he, too, has had sex with Hester. He refuses her offer of an encounter this time, but he makes it quite clear that she was "phenomenal" (44). Later, the Doctor returns and tells her that her "spay" is scheduled for the next day; "You wont feel a thing," he says (85).

Reverend D, the local preacher, has also had sex with Hester and is the father of her youngest child, Baby (he is, in both the script and contemporary colloquialism, "Baby-daddy"). His sermons, which he tapes and sells to his congregation, encourage the impoverished people around him to "pull yrself up" (46). He has crawled out of the gutter, so he says, so of course everyone else can. His benevolence is short-lived, as first he tries to pawn Hester off on social service agencies, then convinces her not to tell the authorities that he is Baby's father, and finally tells her that he will arrange for her to be paid child support.

When Hester returns for her money, he is having his church built, but he has no money to give her, allegedly. He tells her, "I'll take up a collection for you on Sunday," for which she should come back. In the meantime, he asks her to perform oral sex on him, and he tosses her a crumpled bill. It is less than she would make as a prostitute, and as many times as Hester is used sexually by the people who are supposed to help her, one wonders if she would not be better off selling herself rather than giving herself away for almost nothing.

The fourth confession is Reverend D's. He claims that "she threw herself at me," which may in fact be true, but he has the option of refusing her (and helping her instead). When she first tells him that she is pregnant, he gives her money to "take care of it" (79). While incidents with two of the men in Hester's life might well be expected, we expect more from the Welfare, who is also a black woman. As Hester's caseworker, it is her job to help Hester; her help has not exactly been forthcoming. She spends part of her time chastising Hester, "We at Welfare are at the end of our rope with you. We put you in a job and you quit. We put you in a shelter and you walk. We put you in school and you drop out. Yr children are also truant. Word is they steal. Stealing is a gateway to crime, Hester. Perhaps your young daughter is pregnant. Who knows. We build bridges you burn them. We sew safety nets, rub harder, good strong safety nets and you slip through the weave" (54). Welfare also has Hester rub her shoulders and comb her hair; while she does, Hester's underlying anger slips out. "Dont *make* me hurt you," Hester whispers as she combs Welfare's hair. Hester's agitation grows even as Welfare puts her to work doing piecework, sewing. In Welfare's confession, though, we are made aware of the less-than-respectable history between them. The afternoon that Welfare refers to as teaching Hester "manners" was actually spent in a threesome with Welfare and her husband. Once again, the system that is supposed to help her abuses her, both figuratively and literally. It is not so surprising, then, that Hester threatens to hurt Welfare twice.

Even Hester's "friend," Amiga Gringa (White Friend, in Spanish) seeks to sexually exploit Hester. The "friendship" with this white woman has little benefit for Hester and is exploitive. Amiga's plan is to film a girl-on-girl porno that she can then sell for money. She often sells things for Hester, but never gives her all of the money she earns. Amiga spends a lot of time with Jabber, Hester's oldest. Jabber still wets the bed at thirteen, and it is possible that he is being sexually abused by Amiga. Amiga represents an objectifying interest in blackness; she considers herself Hester's friend and claims to help her.

In both *Venus* and *In the Blood*, Parks probes the ways in which black women's sexuality has been represented as deviant; she also exposes the ways in which that perspective has led to both the iconization of black female sexuality in the image of the "Venus Hottentot" and how the effects of that icon affect the lives of contemporary black women (represented by Hester).

"Queen" of Welfare?

Though the image of the black welfare queen dates back at least to the 1960s and the Moynihan Report, it was revived and invigorated in the debates over "welfare reform" in the 1990s.[4] The most drastic changes from AFDC (Aid to Families with Dependent Children) to TANF (Temporary Aid to Needy Families) are "workfare" and the five-year lifetime limit on benefits. The programs billed as "welfare to work" have been critiqued by feminists since they were developed under the Clinton administration. The programs, ideally constituted to give poor women jobs that will take them off welfare rolls, provide some job training and job placement. They do not, however, ensure that clients are placed in positions where they will earn living wages; most of these positions also do not provide childcare or childcare allowances. They are notoriously frustrating for women who would like to work but lack the skills to work in a position that would actually pay them a living wage. Without adequate childcare, the woman is likely to end up either back where she started, or worse off than when she started. A job paying $8.00 an hour brings a *pretax* income of $1280 a month, and $15,360 a year. For a family of three (a woman with two children), this is barely above the federal poverty line ($13,133 for one parent/two children). Considering that most positions provided through TANF lack health care, sick leave, or paid holidays, *and* that this is pretax income, such a position would keep a family like this in poverty. In fact, according to 1998 statistics, 37 percent of children in single-parent families lived in poverty.

Parks's Hester fits the U.S. stereotype of the "welfare queen." As the characters in the prologue say (as do so many people in the United States about people on welfare):

SHOULDN'T HAVE IT IF YOU CANT AFFORD IT
AND YOU KNOW SHE CANT
SHE DON'T GOT NO SKILLS
CEPT ONE
CANT READ CANT WRITE
SHE MARRIED?
WHAT DO YOU THINK?
SHE OUGHTA BE MARRIED
THAT'S WHY THINGS ARE BAD LIKE THEY ARE
CAUSE OF GIRLS LIKE THAT
THAT EVER HAPPEN TO ME YOU WOULDN'T SEE ME
     HAVING IT
YOU WOULDN'T SEE THAT HAPPENING TO ME
WHO THE HELL SHE THINK SHE IS
AND NOW WE GOT TO PAY FOR IT (5)

The cacophony of voices that opens the play reiterates the kinds of comments that are generally made about women on welfare. The juxtaposition of Hester from *The Scarlet Letter* with contemporary welfare queens suggests that we are not far removed from early eighteenth-century Americans in their condemnation of children born out of wedlock.

The condemnation of Hester provides a clue to Hester's situation; a black single mother on welfare does not occupy a position of power in the United States. In the face of her illiteracy, Hester cannot read "SLUT" written up on the wall under the bridge where they live. She is powerless to face the multiple abuses that lay in wait for her: a philandering reverend, a welfare worker who takes Hester to have sex with her husband, and a doctor who wants to sterilize her (or "spay," as Parks uses in the script). As *Boston Globe* critic Ed Siegel says, "In 'In the Blood,' Hester meets with a number of men and women in two hours, each supposedly inhabiting a higher moral universe than that of the illiterate, unemployed young woman, though most of them betray her heedlessly. And each represents an institution—medical, religious, and political—that has abandoned women like Hester in cities all over the country" (Siegel). Her naïveté may be partially to blame for her situation; she believes that others have her best interest, rather than their own, at heart. She continues to trust the institutions that we believe are responsible for helping poor women, but her trust in them reveals the deep hypocrisy of a system that ultimately believes that some people can simply be thrown away.

Hester has slipped through the "safety net" that public assistance is supposed to be. Homeless with five children, she lives under a bridge. She feeds her children "soup" made from scraps unless one of the adults around her gives her a dollar or two. Although she has given the names of her children's fathers to the welfare administration (except the Reverend), they have not found any of them. The Reverend's chastisement of deadbeat fathers shifts decidedly when he is confronted with his own child.

There is also an undercurrent of violence that highlights Hester's communication with her children. Initially, it seems harmless; to stop them from fighting, she calls them all bastards. It is technically true, they are all bastards, but hearing it from their mother makes them all cry. Comments like "go inside and lie down and shut up or you wont see tomorrow" doesn't sound like a significantly hostile statement; black parents have threatened their children with such statements for generations (32). They are usually not meant literally. In this world, however, they are more prophetic than they seem. When Jabber finally reveals to Hester the word that was written on their wall (slut), she beats him to death with a billy club. This act of violence, which occurs near the end of the play, is harsh but understandable; we have been witness to all of the abuse to which Hester has been victim.

Hester says to Welfare, "I dont think the world likes women much." Parks makes explicit the ways in which women are still confined and constrained by a variety of social positions. While Welfare disagrees, she does so from a position of class and educational privilege. Hester is the epitome of the unprivileged: she has no education; she exists on the furthest margins of society; she faces oppression because of her race, her gender, and her class. She does not consider herself blameless for her current position; in fact, she says to Welfare, "My lifes my own fault. I know that. But the world dont help, Maam" (59). She exists in a world that gives her disappointment after disappointment. She is told to pull herself up, but it is impossible for her to do so. Meritocracy clearly does not work in this deconstruction of the American Dream.

Her bludgeoning of Jabber is the violent climax of the play. Jabber is the "speaker" for the other voices—those of the chorus, and of the other characters—his voice is the one that Hester can hear. When Jabber calls her a slut, the outside world's judgment of her comes home. The distance between her and the social institutions represented by the Reverend, the Welfare, and the Doctor is large enough that their admonitions do not fully enter into her reality; she also knows that she is powerless to stop their judgment of her. Jabber, on the other hand, is close. His repeated saying of the word "slut" after Reverend D. has referred to Hester as a "common slut" is the element that cracks Hester's fragile reality. In the

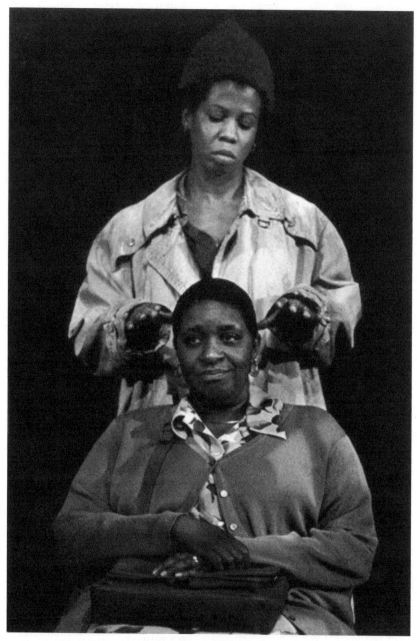

Fig. 4. Kelly Taffe and Isabell Monk in *In the Blood,* Guthrie Theatre, 2001.
Photo by Michael Daniel.

Fig. 5. The cast of *In the Blood*, Guthrie Theatre, 2001. Photo by Michael Daniel.

final confession, Hester vacillates between believing that they were "five mistakes" she should never have had and believing that she "shoulda had a hundred-thousand/ A hundred-thousand a whole *army* full I shoulda!" (107). She is torn between the hypocritical values of society, which structures her children as the key to her powerlessness, and the idea that an "army" of children might have afforded her power. Her final imprisonment is the "big hand coming down on me" that she has felt, and that she expresses as the last lines of the play (110). The "big hand" is inescapable; it is the reality of Hester's life and the institutions that consistently fail her. The life of a woman on welfare is completely removed from the life of a queen, an individual endowed with social and economic power.

"To Leave Here White"

While it is clear that Parks places significant responsibility for the effects of oppression on the oppressors, she also invites the reader/audience member to question whether or not one can be complicit in one's own oppression, and whether the choices that are offered are truly choices. This is most clearly addressed in *Venus;* however, it also appears in *Death of the Last Black Man.*

In the first exchange between the Brother and Venus, he promises her that the streets of London are paved with gold and ultimately convinces her that she should travel with him to make her fortune in England. Their conversation establishes Venus as a "willing" participant in her own oppression. Scene 31 creates for the audience a character in Venus who is obviously a bit naive, but not the exploited woman who was, for all intents and purposes, enslaved. The notion that someone would willingly participate in her own oppression is disconcerting. Black audiences in particular are very uncomfortable with the implication that the play creates Venus as "complicit in her objectification." Adina Porter, who played Venus in the Foreman production, said this about the complicity: "To what extent did the Venus Hottentot (aka Saartjie Baartman, aka '?') have an opportunity to refuse? Her homeland had been vanquished nearly 140 years before her birth, not only by violence and intimidation, but by alien diseases like small pox. Her race was labeled as 'primitive' and legally subjugated as slaves, and her gender was considered 'God's gift of comfort in the wilderness.' She did not have much experience in saying no" (81). Her complicity is measured by her "willingness" to go along with the white men who promise her money if she will accompany them to England. Of course, there have always been those willing to sell themselves (or others) for gold. There were slaves who revealed the planned slave revolts in hopes of gaining favor with whites.

Nevertheless, as Porter commented, Venus did not have much experience saying no; there was really no choice for her, even though she is "presented" with a choice. Her only "choice" is to stay in South Africa as a slave (essentially) or to leave for England to become something other than what she is. Even though she is tricked into thinking that her trip to England is an opportunity and not an order, she does not truly have a choice. Despite the trial in England that decreed that Baartman was not in England against her will, as an audience we must understand that in this instance, Venus is not really complicit in her own oppression. Even if we regard Venus as someone who is able to influence her own destiny by her actions, or if we regard her as an immigrant seeking opportunity elsewhere, it does not change the fact that there is no comparison, for her, between the life she leads in South Africa and the life she might lead in England.

More important, as Venus herself comments, the promise of 50 percent of the take means to her not only that she would no longer have to work, but also "I would have a house. I would hire help. I would be rich. Very rich. Big bags of money" (17). The possibility of returning home wealthy, leaving behind a life of manual labor, is very attractive. With money, returning home is possible; "to go home penniless would be disgraceful" (75).

The appeal of being able to return home in a different social position that one left is part of the American immigrant dream. For Venus, social position is inextricably connected to race; in other words, the idea of not having to work, of being able to hire help, to be very rich, is only possible when one is white. Parks's Venus says to the Chorus of the Court, "I came here black. Give me the chance to leave here white" (76). Not only might money be a motivator, but the concept of leaving one's race behind, of being able to climb to a different social/racial category, is eternally attractive. Venus must perform the European's notion of her in order to achieve success (equated to whiteness).

The possibility of becoming wealthy through performing stereotypes of oneself is not alien to African American culture, but it is usually condemned. In this aspect, Venus does not gain sympathy from black audiences, who cannot help but see her as a kind of sell-out; in other words, it is further evidence of her complicity. The question that Parks implies here is, how do we understand the choices that people make, particularly black women, to agree to exploitation? What are the circumstances that contribute to someone making such a choice? A black feminist aesthetic challenges monolithic constructions of black femininity and highlights the multiple challenges and existential choices that are part and parcel of the intersectionality of gender, race, and class. I am reminded of the situations of many black actors who accepted demeaning roles in both theatre and film in order to become "successful"; I am also reminded of the women who need money to survive and find that they can make more money dancing in a strip club than they can temping in an office. There are no easy answers about agency when such circumstances exist.

The existential choices that face Venus are inflected by race; Parks alludes to the desire to be something other than black in a world in which blackness is vilified. There are hints of this cultural issue, which faces African Americans in the United States, in *Death of the Last Black Man*. Unlike in *Venus*, where these issues are confronted more directly, the inclination to assimilate visually into a white European culture exists as subtle and not-so-subtle comments by the figures in the Chorus. Parks deftly navigates her way through the caricatures and myths that have been created by the "American" culture and works toward re-membering history and subjectivity.

She refers to the characters in *Death* as "figures," rather than as characters. If we consider her development as a playwright moving from more abstract, allegorical dramas to more realistic dramas, *Death* is easily recognizable as an early play. The abstractness and allegory of the play are elements that serve to distance the audience from the characters; her use of Brechtian style constitutes an element of feminist theatre because it does not allow the audience to identify with the characters as real people, but rather to engage them at the level of the political.[5] There are two main characters, Black Man with Watermelons and Black Woman with Fried Drumstick. The exchanges between the two of them constitute the most narrative part of the script. The Black Woman believes that her husband, Black Man with Watermelons, has been killed, but she finds him sitting on the porch. In the process of telling her what has happened to him, we discover that he was lynched (hanged from a tree branch) and also put to death by electrocution (at one point, he is sitting in the electric chair). He has returned to her for traditional burial, and she eventually realizes this and responds.

There are also many other figures in the play; they populate the choral scenes that introduce the play and come between the scenes with Black Woman and Black Man. These figures are elements of African American culture. Queen-then-Pharaoh-Hatshepsut is both history and myth, the only woman to be pharaoh in ancient Egypt. Ham is the "first" black person, turned black in the Old Testament for laughing at his father's nakedness. Old Man River Jordan links "Old Man River," from the Broadway musical *Showboat*, and the River Jordan, associated during slavery with crossing into the promised land (the North).[6] And Bigger and Bigger and Bigger is a reference to Richard Wright's character Bigger Thomas from *Native Son*; Parks's intimation here is that the character Bigger Thomas has grown from a simple character to a larger-than-life stereotype of the big, violent, black man. Before Columbus is a reference to the belief of some Afrocentric scholars that Africans explored the "New World" before Columbus. The characters named for foods are Yes and Greens Black-Eyed Peas Cornbread, and Lots of Grease and Lots of Pork. Both of these names are derived from the traditional diets of African Americans; they also happen to be elements of New Year's Day dinner.[7] The Voice On Thuh Tee V functions as the voice of the dominant culture, perpetuating and further mythologizing Black Man.

These "figures" function to situate the play politically, probing into the myths, histories, and legacies of African American life. Repeatedly, the characters are urged by each other to inscribe their history, one that has been erased and ignored. Yes and Greens Black-Eyed Peas Cornbread says, "You should write it down because if you dont write it down then they will come along and tell the future that we did not exist" (104). The characters write history throughout the play, remembering both historical characters and mythological creations.

Parks's characters are the reflection of black subjectivity as it has been created in the New World. European exploration and colonization have led to the end of the world as it once was and have changed the lives and selves of blacks. Parks deconstructs the racist black/African American identity, particularly in the names of her characters. These Brechtian deconstructions allow for characters like Prunes and Prisms, for example. Prunes and Prisms is an old phrase from African American folklore. Allegedly, repeating the phrase forty times each day would "cure" big lips; for African Americans who wished to erase their race (and achieve "American-ness," which is constructed as white), the big lips that were signs of race could be eliminated. Though this "cure" never actually worked, its existence signifies the process of acculturation to which blacks were subject; whether by straightening one's hair, by applying skin lightener or bleach, or by surgically reducing the size of one's nose, lips, or hips (a contemporary practice), the effort was always towards erasing blackness and assimilating into whiteness. Like Zora Neale Hurston's character in *Color Struck*, many black women experienced self-hate because of the darkness of their skin. Black women used many of the products and processes of attempted assimilation in their efforts to attain the white standards that were imposed on them and to escape the negative images associated with black women.[8]

Parks deconstructs and reconfigures the biblical story of Ham through the figure of "Ham," from whom the black race is supposed to have come.[9] In taking on Ham, Parks takes on the European Christian legitimations of slavery in the Bible. Genesis 9:25–27 states: "Cursed be Canaan! The lowest of slaves will he be to his brothers. He also said, 'Blessed be the Lord, the God of Shem! May Canaan be the slave of Shem. May God extend the territory of Japheth; may Japheth live in the tents of Shem and may Canaan be his slave.'" These verses informed proponents of slavery in the United States; as Sen. James Hammond said, "The doom of Ham has been branded on the form and features of his African descendants. The hand of fate has united his color and destiny. Man cannot separate what God hath joined" (Miller 139).

As part of her play on the story of Ham and its implication in the enslavement of blacks in the United States, Parks also deconstructs the trope of the biblical family tree. In doing so, she reminds her audience that the history of the African American is inextricably tied to her or his association with the slave owner. There are no "proper" names in this revised list of "begats," but instead the names are much like those slaves who were named by their masters or named themselves. It is also a sly remembrance of the rape of black women by slave owners and the difficulties of maintaining family ties when relatives were sold away from each other, "Those strange relations between that thuh mother and Yuh Fathuh thuh son brought forth uh odd lot: called: Yes Massuh, Yes Missy, Yes Maam n Yes Suh Mistuh Suh which goes tuh show that relations with your relations produces complications" (121). While "Prunes and Prisms" as a figure reflects an impulse toward assimilation, the other figures in the play seek a different kind of assimilation: an assimilation of past and future subjectivities and cultures in an effort to reclaim and redefine an African American culture.

The Black Woman Re-Members Culture

It is through the figure of Black Woman with Fried Drumstick that Parks demonstrates the role of the black woman in maintaining the culture and the community. Black Woman initiates this by engaging with Black Man with Watermelons and the deaths of the Last Black Man. The historic and literary deaths of black men collapse into one repeated death. "Yesterday today next summer tomorrow just uh moment uhgoh in 1317 dieded thuh last black man in thuh whole entire world" (102), says Black Woman. "He falls twenty-three floors to his death. 23 floors from uh passin ship from space tuh splat on thuh pavement," referencing the death of Ronald McNair in the 1985 space shuttle *Challenger* accident; he was the United States' only black astronaut at the time (102). Later, Black Man is strapped to an electric chair, obviously symbolic of the propensity for the American legal system to execute black men: "They had theirselves uh extender cord. Fry uh man in thuh town square needs uh extender tuh reach em thuh electric Hookup thuh chair tuh thuh power" (108). He later appears with a rope around his neck dragging a tree branch, a reference to the practice of lynching. Black Woman says to him, "Let me loosen thuh tie let me loosen thuh neck-lace let me loosen up thuh noose that stringed him up let me leave thuh tree branch be" (118). The black feminist subject leaves the tree branch, not forgetting the past, but releasing the pain of injustice.

Black Woman is in one of the historic places of black women, left alive after the unjust deaths of black men. However, the job of Parks's Black Woman is not simply to take care of the burial arrangements; in this case, she must also ensure that there is a burial of the stereotype of the black man; after all, this is not just a black man, but a black man with water-melons. While he is associated with watermelons (just as Black Woman is associated with fried chicken), this Black Man is one who comes with the baggage of racist society. The importance of the Black Man in this play is important to Parks's black feminist aesthetic; Black Woman's concern is not only for her own liberation, but the liberation of the race.

The man who is dead comes back; at first Black Woman thinks that he has escaped, but realizes that is not exactly true. The Black Man has returned for burial and is in a place between life and death, or both life and death, collapsing the Western binaries between those two states. His death is both a death and rebirth; the old constructions of the black male are dying, being buried, leaving a space for the creation of a new subjectivity, one that is created by the individual rather than imposed by society. Death is the path to rebirth of subjectivity. In Parks, what remains is the history and the subject, the Black Woman. The death of Parks's Last Black Man visibly creates subjectivity and voice. The Black Woman turns the dirt, plants him, and re-members him after his historic multiple death. Finally, the Black Man can move his hands; he is no longer imprisoned by the old stereotypes.

These three plays represent a fragment of Parks's work, and they pro-gressively demonstrate a black feminist aesthetic. Parks creates a space within dramatic literature and in theatrical performance that embraces a range of styles, from the abstract "figures" of *Death of the Last Black Man* to the comparatively more realistic characters in *In The Blood*. Unlike the realistic dramas of Cleage, Parks chooses to create allegorical characters through which she can reveal the complexities of representations of black-ness, and more specifically black women, in contemporary culture. The nonlinear, choral forms used in *Death of the Last Black Man* and *Venus* make connections with other dramatic forms, like classical Greek drama, while retaining the general cultural specificity of African American culture and experience, in which the call-and-response and choral forms of the black church play prominent roles. Parks's work provides an artistic bridge from the works of earlier black feminist playwrights who embraced abstract or allegorical forms, from Marita Bonner to Adrienne Kennedy.

5 Kia Corthron's Everyday Black Women

Black feminist playwrights have used drama to address issues of concern in their communities; the theatre has also provided audiences a way to confront the issues brought up in theatrical performance. Kia Corthron is one of the young emergent black women playwrights whose work is rooted in both black feminism and critical race feminism. Corthron's plays have dealt with a range of social justice issues affecting blacks in contemporary society: abortion, the death penalty, police violence, poverty, and war. Her plays are "issue plays"; while they explicitly take on social and political issues, they do not lack story or character. They ask us to consider questions of justice, especially in a U.S. context of racial oppression. In this chapter, I will examine part of Corthron's growing body of work in the context of both black feminism and critical race feminism in the twenty-first century. *Wake Up, Lou Riser* was neither published nor widely produced, but is nonetheless an important work dealing with the historical fact of Klan violence and the continuing search for justice against racist violence. *Breath, Boom* has been published and produced widely; its focus on the life of a young female gang member incorporates violence, sexual abuse, and relationships between mothers and daughters. *Cage Rhythm,* though earlier, is almost a precursor; its focus is on women in prison. *Cage Rhythm* was initially produced with *Come Down Burning;* it engages the issue of abortion and the difficulties faced by poor, rural women in trying to control their reproductivity. *Splash Hatch on the E Going Down* incorporates some of the devices she used in *Lou Riser* to explore teen pregnancy and environmental issues. In all of these plays, Corthron takes on issues that are explicitly black feminist ones.

The issue of justice has been the most recent trajectory in the development of black feminist thought, particularly critical race feminism. Critical race feminism engages feminism through legal scholarship and legal theory.

The issues of critical race feminists are very much the issues that are engaged in Corthron's plays. Adrien Katherine Wing describes critical race feminism as anti-essentialist, multidisciplinary research, engaged in both theory and practice. In particular, it engages the issues of motherhood and single-parenthood, which are prominent in *Splash Hatch* and *Come Down Burning.* Additionally, she explores crime and criminality and its effects on black women, as are taken up in *Breath, Boom,* and issues of social and economic justice, all of which play roles in all of Corthron's plays. These plays highlight and creatively reiterate the historic situation of black women within U.S. culture. The plays critique the failures of a liberal democratic society, particularly how society has failed people who are disadvantaged because of both race and gender.

Lynching and Justice: *Wake Up, Lou Riser*

Ostensibly, *Wake Up, Lou Riser* is a play about four young black women and a member of the Ku Klux Klan. Through the presentation of this story, the situation of these young women focuses our attention not only on historical circumstances but also on the function of justice, and the questions about issues of justice within a racist and sexist culture. Ultimately, this play enables the audience to question justice, both the seeking of justice and the possibilities for the realization of justice in a racist and sexist context. *Wake Up, Lou Riser* was produced at Circle Rep Lab in 1992 and received the Delaware Theatre Company's Connections Award in 1996.[1]

Wake Up, Lou Riser portrays an event that one might expect in the 1880s or '90s, but is set in the present (1990s). The play is written in three scenes.[2] In Scene 1, five black youths, who range in age from twelve to their mid-twenties, are staying alone while their parents are away at a wedding. There is only one boy, Owen, who is a high school senior. His sisters are Boot, his closest sibling, who is a year behind him; Anj, the eldest; Trace, the next oldest; and Cory, who is twelve. Owen is outraged at the Ku Klux Klan rally that is taking place in their southern town the next day. He wants to make a statement, and he and Boot decide that they will impersonate klansmen and infiltrate the rally. Trace has encouraged them and jokingly agrees to make their outfits for them.

This is not the first time Owen and Boot have attended a Klan event, for as we discover early in the play, they had gone to the previous year's rally and cross burning up on a local hill. Hidden by darkness, Owen and Boot watch the entire event from a few feet away. Owen is no longer threatened by them: "Cuza all the horror stories 'bout 'em, my spine did tingle when I first seen those hoods. But after that: they was nothin'. Boot and me gaggin' ourselves so we don't laugh out loud" (8). Therefore, he feels that any infiltration by himself and Boot (for they do most things together) could not possibly bring any harm to them. Owen is, however, very serious about stopping the Klan parade. Anj is the only one of the siblings who opposes the infiltration plan. The scene ends with Anj's objection and Trace's agreement to help. At a crucial point during the march, Owen plans that he and Boot will leave the march for the sidelines, remove the gloves that hide their race, and raise their fists in a black power salute.

The second scene is the rally, where we meet Lou Riser, head of the local Klan, and a variety of other klansmen and women including Mrs. Grey, the high school English teacher, and Rodney, who has only recently graduated from their high school. Boot and Owen arrive at the rally wearing their hoods, of course, so that they are not identified as black. They are the only ones wearing hoods. Out of a sense of pride in Klan membership, we learn, the members no longer wear hoods. Owen's plans hinged upon his understanding of the workings of the Klan. The no-hoods rule makes it impossible for them to "hide" among the Klan members because it is obvious that they are not regular members. They call even more attention to themselves by their crude robes and their seemingly formal gloves. There is so much interest in them that Owen has to spend a significant amount of time talking to Klan leader Riser. He has to explain that he and Boot are from Virginia (which is why they are wearing gloves).

Owen is also exposed to the various philosophies of these Klan members; they are not unitary, and some are quite different from what he has imagined. Of all the members, Mrs. Grey is the most "reasonable"; she opposes the more contemporary, violent racist organizations. "Separation is one thing, violence, brutality—something else. I don't go for it" (31). Rodney keeps insisting that Owen and Boot remove their hoods, but his elders let the siblings slide. It looks like they will get away with their plan, but as the march begins, a little girl (who had been walking around with a small black doll hanging from a noose on a stick) pulls Owen's hood off his head. He is identified, and he and Boot run away. Mrs. Grey, the pacifist, says, "Hope that was the funniest joke you ever pulled. Nigger. Wait" (37).

When the third scene of the play opens, we discover Cory, dressed in a black cape and hood (reverse Klan attire), and we hear Lou Riser's screams from offstage. The girls bring him blindfolded into the space. The audience sees that Boot carries a pistol, Trace has a knife, and Anj has a rope, which she tosses over a tree branch and forms a noose. They proceed to threaten and torture Riser throughout the scene. Through the torture, we discover that the missing sibling, Owen, had been taken from his room and murdered by the Klan. Riser at first denies any role in Owen's death, but eventually gives the sisters what they want: a confession—but only after they put his head in the noose and are ready to pull the chair out from under him. The meaning of the play's title is revealed, because when the Klan members came to get Owen, they told him, "Wake up, Owen Kaylor." Riser recounts the murder, and at the end of his recounting, the sisters yank the chair out from under him.

Before Riser is fatally injured, the sisters change their minds about killing him. Cory grabs Riser's body and holds it so that it is no longer hanging, and it is revealed that Riser is not dead, but only unconscious. They must then debate what they could possibly do at this point. If they kill him, they will likely be found out; if they let him live, he can certainly identify them. They decide to take the risk of being identified, cut Riser down, and leave him.

In many ways, this play follows in a tradition of antilynching plays written by both black and white women.[3] In antilynching plays of the 1920s and 1930s, the young men are either lynched before they can be saved, or are saved at the last moment by the intercession of a powerful white man. In none of them are the black women (who are those who remain) able to pursue justice for the murder of their husband/son/grandson. However, in this play, the contemporary remaining victims (the sisters) are able to strike back, even if to a limited degree. The situation of the Kaylor sisters reflects the historic situations of women of African descent in the United States.

In cases that involved the Klan, the legal system has been notoriously slow in even bringing suspected murderers to trial, when it has acted at all. To cite one recent example, it took nearly forty years for the last living Klan member responsible for the bombing of the Sixteenth Street Baptist Church in Birmingham, Alabama, in which four young women were killed, to be tried and found guilty. Corthron chooses to have the Kaylor sisters respond to their brother's murder with violence, rather than waiting for the legal system. She also has them choose not to kill him.

Corthron's dramaturgical choice points out that the law is not in favor of the oppressed. The Kaylor family has no recourse within a legal system that has, historically, demonstrated this point. Though our icon of Justice is blindfolded, the actual practice of law has not been blind to race. The foundation of law, residing in liberalism, carries into its use the racism that undergirds it. It carries the belief that people are judged as individuals, and that the system is blind to race, gender, or class. The ideology of liberalism (equality, individuality) reveals itself to be a myth; it is believed that differences among individuals have no bearing on their political or legal status. However, race and gender as categories retain a central place within culture, and those categories have bearing on the political and legal status of individuals.

The practical effects of liberalist ideology are evidenced by the legal system's long-standing inability to prosecute Klan members for murder. Within the play, the Klan's murder of Owen is also expected to go unpunished, echoing more than a century of unpunished violence against blacks in the United States by white mobs. The sisters also feel the effects. Part of their decision to cut Riser down from his noose lies in the knowledge that they are more likely to be prosecuted for his murder than Riser to be prosecuted for Owen's. It also implies that the value of Riser's life is more highly valued than that of Owen, or of his sisters.

These circumstances point out boldly the historical predicament of blacks when faced with mob violence from whites. Not only were blacks more likely prosecuted, they were also more heavily penalized when prosecuted for crimes against whites; this remains the case. Whites were essentially immune from prosecution in lynching cases until 1968 (as Cory states in the play). Within the legal/justice system of the United States, particularly in the South (where the play takes place), there is little precedent for the prosecution of this kind of murder. Consider how long it took for the murderers of Medgar Evers, Denise McNair, Addie Mae Collins, Carole Robertson, and Cynthia Wesley to be prosecuted successfully.[4] Several other cases involving the murders of civil rights activists remain unsolved and are likely to remain so as witnesses age, forget, or die.

As an audience, we understand that because of the alleged lack of evidence against the Klan members, the legal system will once again fail to act in the Kaylors' favor by prosecuting Owen's murderer(s). The town has acted in bad faith, knowing who is responsible but behaving as though it does not. Because we understand the historic situation of the legal system and its historic lack of prosecution of those who lynch, it makes sense that the only alternative is for the sisters to act and to become the moral law that acts against the murder. Lou Riser is only punishable by the victims of his crime, Owen's sisters. They act as judge, jury, and executioner, and ultimately even as the governor providing a last-minute stay of execution.

Historically, black women in the United States have needed to act outside the law because it denies them justice because of their race and gender. Many historical texts written about black women in the United States elucidate the struggles against violence. Angela Davis's *Women Race and Class,* Paula Giddings's *When and Where I Enter,* and Gerda Lerner's *Black Women in White America,* as well as an entire genre of antilynching plays, all recount the exasperating circumstances of black women who were unable to prosecute the white men who had perpetrated violence against them. The historical reality demonstrates the tacit acceptance of lynching, and the perpetrators of such horrors were known yet rarely prosecuted.[5] Black women could not appeal to the legal system, but rather were required to either live with the results of such violence or find ways outside of conventional legal methods to exact justice.

The Kaylor sisters act outside the law in order to seek justice. But what exactly is justice, in this case? The play asks us as an audience to consider the meaning of justice in an unjust system. On an existential level, as the third act opens and the play reaches its climax, the audience is implicated in the sisters' decision and in the murder of Owen. We understand the sisters' inclination to treat their brother's murderer the way he was treated, and their desire not for punishment but retribution. Historically, black women have not had the "satisfaction" of either punishment for perpetrators or retribution from them. The Kaylor sisters occupy a place where they may not have the opportunity to have Riser and the Klan legally punished, but they might be able to exact retribution—an eye for an eye, torture for torture, murder for murder. We also understand, as an audience, that their vigilante "justice" can never truly be justice. What might be the appropriate punishment for Riser? Is it the death penalty? In other words, do we feel that the sisters are justified in their attempt to kill Riser, even for a moment? As we consider these questions in the context of the play, they resonate strongly (especially at the beginning of the twenty-first century) about the larger issues of justice, "punishment," and retribution.

Reshaping Teen Motherhood: *Splash Hatch*

In addition to issues of criminal justice, the issue of teen pregnancy is also an important one for black feminists. The United States has the highest rate of teen pregnancy among developed nations. It is also true that there are particular beliefs and stereotypes about teens who become pregnant; teen pregnancy is most often considered endemic to the inner cities, and therefore to young black and Latina women, or to poor rural women, specifically poor whites. Common notions about pregnant teens are that they are not intelligent (or they would not have become pregnant in the first place), or that they lack two-parent families (leaving them without the model of the nuclear family).

The stereotypes are not completely without substance. The rate of births for teens with less than seven years of schooling is 33 percent, compared to only 5 percent for teens with more than seven years of schooling. Part of the difference can be attributed to the likelihood of a more highly educated teen to choose the option of abortion rather than carry a pregnancy to term; it is also more likely that they have parents with more than seven years of schooling, and who emphasize the importance of education.[6]

Table 1. Teen Fertility Rates in Five "Developed" Countries

Country	Fertility rate per 1,000 women aged 15–19
France	82
Germany	112
Great Britain	292
Japan	42
Poland	262
United States	572

Note: Most current data on pregnancies of young women aged 15–19: in 2001, there were 145,324 births; in 2000, the number of births was 157,209 and total number of pregnancies was 281,900. Clearly, there has been a decrease in teen pregnancies in the U.S., but the U.S. still lags behind other developed countries in fertility rate.

Year AGI report published: 1998. Rates are for 0–3 years prior to the survey except where otherwise noted.

In developed countries, the rate is for the most recent year available — 1992 in Great Britain (England and Wales only) and 1993–95 elsewhere.

Source: AGI, Into a New World: Young Woman's Sexual and Reproductive Lives, New York: AGI, 1998. *Notes on data sources:* www.agi-usa.org/tablemaker/inw-data-sources.mhtml. *Survey years:* France, 1994; Germany, 1992; Great Britain, 1991; Japan, 1992; Poland, 1991; United States, 1995.

That the concept of the disinterest of inner-city single-parent families has an effect on public policy is clear in the legislation surrounding welfare programs (both AFDC and TANF). One element of TANF in Michigan, the "Learnfare" program, punished mothers on welfare for their childrens' absences from school; this is one solid example. "Perhaps the most fundamental conceptual flaw of Learnfare is its assumption that the problem of social deviancy is endemic to a child's family, rather than a function of external sources"[7] (Augustin 146).

In *Splash Hatch on the E Going Down,* Corthron seeks to broaden the audience's idea of teen pregnancy and parenthood by creating two black teenage female characters, both of whom are pregnant. Thyme is pregnant for the first time, while Shaneequa is on her second pregnancy. Though the girls are close friends, their situations are somewhat different. Thyme is "married" to the father of her baby; Erry (for Eric) lives with Thyme and her parents. While Erry has "taken an early retirement from high school," Thyme is still in school. Thyme is also an avid reader, while Erry has great difficulty reading. Shaneequa is pregnant by the father of her first child, but by the time she is ready to deliver her second child, she is seeing Ahmed.

Thyme and Shaneequa also defy stereotypes by being dedicated students. Thyme spends as much time as she can in the library; she is a straight-A student. Shaneequa is not as obsessive about learning as Thyme, but she is painfully aware that having children detracts from her abilities as a student. She cannot participate in track and field, and her studies are interrupted by lack of sleep or lack of child care, "Jus' wait 'til the time morning sickness make you miss the math test. Call Mr. Davis, beg him letcha make it up nex' day, he say okay. But nex' day your mother got a doctor's appointment, your aunt ain't home, you got no babysitter. Come in day after, tryin' not to cry, tell him 'I meant to take the makeup test yesterday, no babysitter.' And he look at you like that's the dumbest excuse he ever heard in his whole entire life" (*Splash Hatch* 22).

It is surprising to some audiences that "smart" teens could get pregnant and choose to carry their children to term. It is part of American cultural "baggage" that the stereotype of the welfare recipient is an inner-city, black, or Latina single mother who was first pregnant as a teenager and who probably did not finish high school (of course, it is true that this describes many teen mothers, but not all). Corthron's presentation of a teen mother who defies most expectations is not easy for some audiences to accept. Corthron discovered this during a run of the show in Baltimore:

> Most of the subscribers who came to the luncheon were middle-aged white persons, and they got the information that the central character was a very bright teenager and that she was pregnant, and they became threatened by the idea. They kept saying, "Well, how could she be smart? A smart girl would not get pregnant." They started talking disparagingly about girls having babies and their parents having to raise them. I was saying that the girl's parents are not going to throw her out in the street; they want her to go to college, and she is raising her own child. (A. Greene 94)

That this audience (and probably others) had difficulty imagining this as a "realistic" representation of a young black woman is indicative of the ways in which those stereotypes persist. Corthron's choice further demonstrates her feminism. She is creating the possibility that Thyme could be a "good mother" even though she lacks the elements of identity that tend to make one a "good mother," that is, race, class, and education that are not currently hers. Thyme's desire to be a good mother is also signified by her relentless pursuit of knowledge about pregnancy, childbirth, and nursing. She even decides that she will have a water birth based on her research. For a surgical birth, she is all too aware of the perceptions she will have to battle. "You, me, look at us they'll make their conclusions, prejudgements, nothing but some stupid fifteen-year-old projects teenagers they'll assume it. Well real quick they'll find out I'm not stupid and I'm not projects," she asserts to Shaneequa (21).

Living an Environmental Nightmare

While it seems that Thyme has the things that she needs to survive as a young parent—two parents who are at home, a husband who is young but has a job—she is also plagued by the fact that living in Harlem is living an environmental nightmare. Evidence of this fact is as central to the play as the recoding of the "pregnant teenager" stereotype. In the last ten years, both the inhabitants and environmentalists have been made increasingly aware of the environmental threats that exist in places where low-income and minority people live. As Robert Bullard, Glenn Johnson, and Beverly Wright note, "Many economically impoverished communities and their inhabitants are exposed to greater health hazards in their homes, on the jobs, and in their neighborhoods when compared to their more affluent counterparts" (63). It is little wonder that when we first encounter Thyme, she is avidly pursuing knowledge about the environment; she is already confronting three crucial elements of the health hazards of living in Harlem.

The first of these elements is the asthma that plagues Shaneequa. Thyme even attempts to "educate" Shaneequa (as she is wont to do on any subject in which she feels she has expertise) about asthma: "The high incidence of asthma in Harlem is related to the high concentration of exhaust fumes which is related to the great number of city buses which is related to the great number of city bus terminals. There are eight city bus terminals in Manhattan. Seven are in Harlem" (22). Of course, only part of the problem is related to exhaust fumes; there are also irritants like ozone, particulate matter, and sulfur dioxides, as well as allergies to insects like cockroaches. We cannot be sure that Shaneequa's delivery of a stillborn baby is related to her asthma, but it is a possibility.

Corthron also addresses a contemporary controversy in this play. In Act II, Scene 1, Thyme and Shaneequa are sitting at a city park that sits next to a waste treatment plant. As Thyme says, "This [park] is payoff, bribe, this our kids running, sucking in toxic air cuz the white neighborhoods sure didn't wana be looking at it" (37). The waste treatment plant was located not in the most convenient place, which would have been closer to midtown, but rather in the community where people would be least likely to organize against it. Thyme is very conscious about the problems in the New York City environment, and has even done a school project where she notes, "The Environmental Defense Fund estimates that 75% of New York City children under age six have levels of lead in their bodies high enough to cause some permanent brain damage" (23).

All of Thyme's "book learning" is not enough to allow her to see reality, however. Erry, who is working at a fast-food job when the play begins, hears about a job working for a demolition crew that will make him twice as much money. He gets the job, and he brings home a sheet about environmental hazards; one of them is lead poisoning. Because of the age of the buildings being demolished, and because Erry's job involves cleaning up the demolished buildings, he is at very high risk for inhaling lead dust. Because of his limited education, he is not really able to read and understand the hazard pamphlet, and his employers count on the employees not reading it.

Thyme knows quite a bit about lead poisoning, but when Erry begins to suffer the effects of it, she refuses to admit that it is a possibility. Erry is still waiting for his health benefits, which will not commence until after he has worked for six months. He starts feeling ill five weeks after beginning the job, and Thyme is willing to believe that he has the flu. At the same time that Erry's illness is beginning to show, the fine white powder Erry brings home with him on his clothes has begun to collect around Thyme's room. Erry begins showing other symptoms, which worries Thyme's father, Ollie; he worries about Erry "leavin' my daughter a baby and alone" (35).

Four months later, Erry is having seizures in his sleep, and Thyme understands that lead is the culprit, even while she refuses to admit it. Her denial of the fact of Erry's illness is convenient because it enables her to avoid facing Erry's inevitable death. Shaneequa catches her in her self-deception, but neither Erry nor Thyme will do anything about Erry's obvious illness until his insurance begins. Even then, Erry worries about going to the doctor; "no, they don't like that, suspicious, they fire people for that" (43). Erry finally consents, but by then it really is too late. They try chelation therapy, which works for a while, but Erry dies of lead poisoning.

Come Down Burning: Life, Death, and Abortion

From the inner city life of Thyme and Shaneequa to the rural poverty of Skoolie and Tee, Corthon's worlds engage the different types of poverty that exist in the United States. In *Come Down Burning*, Corthron takes on one of the most visible issues of feminists, but one that is not as visible among black feminists. Abortion is and has been an issue for black feminists as early as Anna Julia Cooper; it can also be measured by the inclusion of Faye Wattleton in *Re/Membering Aunt Jemima* and Cleage's play *Blues for an Alabama Sky*, where it figures prominently. Corthron was inspired by the threat to *Roe v. Wade* in the late 1980s and early 1990s. "I wanted to address that [fragility of Roe], because I feel that wealthy women can always get abortions, but the poor have to go to dangerous means" (A. Greene 89).

Come Down Burning addresses both the past and the future. Upon first read, one might think that its setting is in the early twentieth century, when abortion was illegal, and when it was necessary to perform abortions without medical care or support. In this, Corthron's play imagines what the future of reproductive rights may be if abortion is made illegal. However, the presence of a hot plate, phone, and ambulance reveal a nonspecific time, but one that is certainly not early to mid-twentieth century.

Skoolie and Tee live in an impoverished rural area in the South. Skoolie, who is partially paralyzed, is responsible for her sister Tee and Tee's three children. Skoolie pushes herself around on a cart; it gets her where she most needs to go. Skoolie manages to wheel herself across the street to the general store and around her "house," a renovated shack. Her income comes from the abortions she performs on local women. She cannot afford a wheelchair. Tee works as a dishwasher in a diner, where she almost makes enough money to get by. The fathers of Evie and Will-Joe are in and out of town, and their lives, and are not sufficiently reliable to provide Tee any assistance in raising them. The infant, Jazzman, has stopped taking Tee's milk, and Skoolie deduces that Tee is pregnant again.

Skoolie's best friend Bink is also one of her customers. Bink returns to town after having been away and is unexpectedly pregnant. Bink and her husband already have two children and do not want any more. Though Skoolie takes an opportunity after the successful abortion of Bink's baby to warn, "hope you and Gary be wearin' the proper equipment in the future," Bink is not ignorant of birth control (439). "We was always careful, Skoolie, nothin' a hundred percent" (439). Indeed, Bink is correct, and her type of abortion—because of failed birth control—comprise the majority of abortion procedures in the United States.[7] Of course, the procedure is confidential; after all, as Skoolie says, "I think I like to stay outa jail" (429).

While Bink's procedure is successful, Corthron does not let us off so easily. Tee's pregnancy is a problem for the family; they have just enough to get by, with Skoolie styling hair and performing the occasional abortion, and Tee has already lost two infants to ill health. It is clear to Skoolie that they cannot afford to have another child in the house, particularly as Jazzman is still nursing (he is only three months old). Tee seems to be avoiding Skoolie's request:

> SKOOLIE: Tee, ya can't . . . not think about it. Jus' can't . . . jus' can't have another baby, not think 'bout no options. We's hungry.
> TEE: I know, Skoolie, I ain't thinkin' 'bout it cuz I know, cuz I know not much choice. *I gonna pull it out* [italics mine]. (431)

From Tee's choice of words, we have a clue about the outcome. Indeed, in the last scene of the play, we realize that Tee has attempted to abort the child herself and has been unsuccessful. She is bleeding profusely, goes into shock, and dies.

Tee's death is unnecessary; if she had allowed Skoolie to perform the abortion, she would probably have lived. More important, though, is that if she had access to health care and did not live in an impoverished community that has no legal abortion provider, she might have been able to obtain contraceptives (free or at low cost with certain clinics), or to have a legal abortion done. Corthron reminds us of the human toll of illegal abortion with Tee's death; before the legalization of abortion, "80 percent of deaths caused by illegal abortions involved Black and Puerto Rican women" (Ross 155). It is not only the overturning of *Roe v. Wade* that is dangerous to poor, especially rural, women's health. The 1989 *Webster* Supreme Court decision "banned the use of public employees or facilities for performing abortions not necessary to save the mother's life" (Roberts 285–86). Because she is poor and would likely use federal Medicare, she would have to pay for the abortion herself, because the Hyde amendment does not reimburse the costs of abortions. The number of abortion providers (and indeed the number of physicians trained in basic first-trimester procedure) shrinks yearly, and there are many areas—like the rural mountainous region where Skoolie and Tee live—where it might be necessary to travel more than two hundred miles to find a legal provider. While we might want to think of the world of this play as an imagined world, it is stark reality for millions of poor women, particularly poor women of color, in the United States.

Shedding Light on Girls and Gangs

Breath, Boom, Corthron's most produced play to date, takes as its subject female gang members and the roots and causes of violence in U.S. culture.[8] The protagonist, Prix, is the leader of a small female gang; the play follows her from age sixteen to age thirty, tracking her relationships with friends, fellow gang members, and her mother. One of Corthron's motives in writing the play was to examine violence and emphasize the fact that violence does not emerge out of a vacuum. In an interview with Lenora Inez Brown, Corthron says, "I don't believe that children become violent in a vacuum. The character Cat also mentions that in the play. Many are quick to judge young people and youth violence and want to try kids who get into trouble as adults. Nobody is looking at the root of the problem to see where that violence comes from. As the statistics show (and as Cat spouts), the violence committed by adults against young people is exponentially greater than the other way around" (54).

The issue of girls' involvement in gangs has been growing as the numbers of gangs have increased. "Although there is insufficient data, it is estimated that 10 percent to 30 percent of the entire gang population is female. Some of these women are members of all-female gangs, which are found in nearly every large city. Female gangs tend to be smaller and more dispersed than male gangs" (Wing and Willis 244). There are many reasons why teen girls join gangs; as Wing and Willis note, "Gangs supply the family-like relationships, emotional support, and social controls that are lacking in many poverty-stricken urban communities" (245). This is evident in the life of Prix, Angel, Malika, and Comet, who comprise a kind of family in the midst of the dysfunctional biological families in which they live.

Corthron also chooses to have Prix be a survivor of sexual abuse. Her mother's boyfriend, Jerome, began molesting her when she was only five years old. Her mother, who is an addict, has remained oblivious to Jerome's abuse of Prix even while she herself has been physically abused by Jerome. Again, from Wing and Willis, "a girl's involvement in crime may be linked to the girl's undocumented status as a victim of physical and sexual abuse" (246). Prix's violence is a learned behavior, because she has lived in a violent environment almost all of her life; she goes from a home in which both she and her mother are abused to prison, and in both places violence is present all around her.

Prix is an "O.G." at the beginning of the play; she is the "original gangster" or leader of her girl gang, and it is she who controls the members of her gang. Girl gangs in U.S. cities are structured in a few basic ways. As Sudhir Alladi Venkatesh writes, a street gang is commonly defined as "an organized social group governed by a leadership structure, having goals and means of obtaining them that may not be legal or socially sanctioned, and seeking to realize the interests of its individual members as well as the needs of the group" (689). They can be "independent" gangs, comprised only of young women, who may or may not be involved in "delinquent" activities. Other gangs are linked, socially and often economically, with dominant male street gangs. Finally, girls may be involved in gangs by being female members or sexual partners of male gangs. These three different configurations mean very different things for the young women involved. For example, in Prix's gang, members are "jumped in" by being beaten up by several other members of the gang. In gangs where women are part of male street gangs, they are often "rolled in," a process in which they roll dice to see how many of the gang members they must have sex with in order to join. As Venkatesh's article reveals, the reasons for the development of "girl gangs" are numerous, but their origins are connected to protecting the women in the community from domestic violence; to assisting each other with child care, employment opportunities; and to redistribution of money earned in the underground economy (especially sales of illegal drugs).

It does appear that Prix's gang is either one group of a larger female gang, or it is a gang that has maintained an economic association with a male gang. This can be assumed because Prix receives directions about hits and drug deals from someone by phone, but we never know who these people are. Prix has control of her group, that is certain. She coordinates the beating of Comet when Comet tries to get out of the gang in the first scene of the play. Comet is aware that her age (she is turning eighteen) means that her illegal activities will now qualify her for serious jail time rather than juvenile hall. Comet makes the mistake of stating her desire to leave the gang rather than leaving quietly, and she must be punished for it. Prix must publicly punish Comet in order to maintain her position of power within the gang.

The activities of the girls reflect the everyday activities of inner-city girls—Comet takes care of her two-year-old child, Angel and Malika braid each other's hair, Prix makes pipe-cleaner fireworks sculptures. These intersect with the gang activities, such as the drive-by shooting they are planning. It is a perplexing mix of the requirements of their lives and their hopes and aspirations: Malika wants to be a flight attendant, and Prix wants to design fireworks displays. The careless ways in which they discuss the drive-by ("Nothin' personal anyway, just a drive-by, not like we shootin' anybody face-to-face," says Angel), or play with razor blades in their mouths, demonstrate the degree to which violence has become normalized in their lives—as normal as braiding hair or taking care of children (8).

The violence shown or foretold by the girls is sharply highlighted in the first scene of the play by the violence of Prix's home life. After Comet is beaten, Prix's mother and Jerome have two arguments separated by a bout of sexual activity. Prix has been living with this kind of violence for years. Mother's life highlights the lives of many battered women: "You think I wanted it? I got the restrainin' order! I got it, fourteen years! Fourteen years dumb! Fourteen years I been puttin' up with it, finally I wise up, restrainin' order, six months it been effect, how many times he been here that six months? Seven! And I called the police first four times, him bangin' the door down. Slow as they is, and Jerome skilled with a paper clip, no problem he pick the lock 'fore they come, if they come why bother?" (11–12). Not only has Mother been dealing with Jerome's physical abuse for fourteen years, but Prix has been living in an abusive environment as well. Now, she is old enough (and tough enough) to defend herself against him. Shortly after this scene, Mother kills Jerome and is sentenced to prison.

Jerome's death is not an isolated incident; indeed, the lives of Prix and her gang sisters are ones in which violent death is ever-present, and hope has evaporated. In one of the most moving moments in the play, Angel looks through a scrapbook she has collected for years. It recounts the deaths of many friends — six total. They include her big brother Vince, who was an honor roll student, and Terri, who was shot in a drive-by when she was eight.

Prix's gang life continues while she is in prison, but as she ages, the violence in her life decreases. Jerome's ghost returns to be her conscience; he chastises her for not visiting her mother in jail and for still being involved with gang life at age twenty-four. Corthron chooses Jerome deliberately; her "rehabilitation" of this character shows the lengths that Prix must still go to move out of her life of violence. Comet is also "still on the payroll," and stays there because "welfare sure don't cut it. I gotta gangbang supplemental income for the luxuries: food. Diapers" (30). For women who remain involved with gang activities into their twenties, it is often because they need the "supplemental" income they can get from small jobs for larger gangs, including hiding drugs and weapons. As Venkatesh notes, "Money accumulated from the sales of cocaine, heroin, and marijuana and the revenues redistributed by set leaders facilitated purchase of food, groceries, and diapers, as well as the latest fashion commodities" (684).

Four years later, at twenty-eight, Prix begins to leave gang life after she is beaten up by Jupiter, who is Comet's daughter and now a juvenile gang leader. The cycle of violence is continued in Jupiter; Comet has not been much of a mother to her. "My mother fuck! Like I ever see the bitch between jail and the fosters good! And each time I'm took away she wanna bawl and bawl like she so Christ fuckin' sad fuck her! Don'tcha be mentionin' her fuckin' stupid name to me. Don't be bringin' up no goddamn Comet!" (38–39). Obviously, Comet's gang activity (and by extension Jupiter's gang activity) has created Jupiter, who is angry at her mother for not being a good mother to her.

Corthron leaves us hopeful at the end of the play. Prix, while having a picnic with Angel, encounters a woman, Jo, whom she paralyzed earlier (although we do not know exactly how). The woman's anger at Prix is vitriolic, and Prix is both shocked and apologetic. Prix also realizes both the effects of her violence and the fact that she cannot "fix" what she has harmed. She does not even remember what she did, and Jo torments her further by not revealing the exact incident in which she was harmed. Prix's final transformation is agreeing to meet her HIV-infected mother by the Empire State Building, where they begin to create a positive mother-daughter relationship.

Performing Violence: Phenomenology and Semiotics

Corthron provides us with both retold violence and staged violence. As an audience, particularly as a U.S audience likely familiar with representations of violence through film and television, we might be "immune" from the immediacy of seeing violence on stage. Phenomenologically, however, the staging of violence (and the pain that results from violence) "invades, and is in turn invaded by, the perceptual actuality of pain in a way that foregrounds the uncanny circuitry and ambiguity of dramatic representation itself" (Garner 45). In other words, the staging of violence, as real people in the presence of real actors, highlights both the violence and the fact that the performance is not a performance of violence but a representation of the performance of violence. This is true not only of the watching of actual violence, but also in the hearing of violence described or retold.

Riser's description of Owen's murder in *Wake Up, Lou Riser* is a chilling account, made more immediate by the fact that the audience watches as the actor playing Riser stands on a chair with a noose around his neck, and the Kaylor sisters stand around the chair ready to pull it out from under him. Under duress, he relates:

> pull you outa bed nigger scream monkey scream slap them 'cuffs twelve-year p'lice force 'cuffs slap on ya sweat blackie scream cry I kick you in your fuckin' black balls I slap slap you knock aroun' your fuckin' black fuckin' ugly face ape face blood all over it let's tie you to the backa the pick-up awhile drive aroun' drag your ass aroun' blood black red body, rope 'roun' your neck gun to your head we pullin' a trick, cock the trigger to your head move it last second and shoot away but you scream cry like you think we got anything less than the noose intended for you. (57)

After the sisters cut him down and he regains consciousness, he continues his "confession": "Dragged him back of a pick-up for a mile, beat him, kick him, hard to find a place on his face not bruised, bleedin'. Both, and . . . rope 'round his neck, I'm puttin' it around, thinkin' he out cold and the rascal digs his teeth way into my finger, way into the Jesus bone break the skin, break the bone Jesus . . . Strong man" (63). When Corthron wrote this play, she had no way of knowing how prescient this image would be. Today, the image created by Riser in this recounting brings another image to mind for an audience, that of the murder of James Byrd Jr., who was beaten, tied up, and dragged behind a pickup truck in Jasper, Texas, in 1998.[9] The fact of James Byrd's death reminds us that, even in this play about an imagined event, racist violence and murder are still a reality for blacks in the United States.

An onstage hanging also occurs in *Breath, Boom*. Prix sits emotionless while her cellmate, Cat, cheerfully makes a noose out of her bedsheet and throws it over a pipe in their cell. Cat is unable to handle life in jail. While she initially complains about the clothes (she is allowed only five outfits), it is clear that she wants to "belong," but is repeatedly hassled by other girls in jail. Cat is in jail for prostitution, and though she would like to be a gang member, she is not. She is beaten by other girls and knows that it will continue. She has clearly lost touch with reality just before she completes her noose:

> Supper tonight, I seen her people, them girls follows her around, she weren't there guess they threw her in the bean. I come to her girls, say, "Your friend ask me what my name is. My name's Cat." But soon as I say "Your friend ask me what my name is" they start laughtin' so hard I think they don't hear the second part, so I keep sayin' it louder but the louder I say it the louder they laugh. "My name is Cat!" (Giggles) "MY NAME IS CAT!" (giggles, stands on the upper bunk). (25–26)

Prix tells her to jump, and there is a blackout. Unlike with Lou Riser, we do not see Cat take the dive off the bunk. Of course, we have already witnessed other violence; in addition, Cat actually dies, whereas Riser is saved by the sisters.

Of course, there is plenty of other staged violence in *Breath, Boom*. There are the beatings of both Comet, at the beginning of the play, and of Prix by Jupiter and her girls, near the end of the play. In both, the victims lie bloody on the stage. Prix's defense against Jerome features a razor blade at Jerome's neck. The violence is not restricted to that which is actualized on stage; there are also the tales of Fuego's sister's "rolling in" the gang, which requires a gang rape, and Prix's revelation to us that she was raped by Jerome when she was five. We also hear Prix's mother being beaten by Jerome.

In both *Breath, Boom* and *Wake Up, Lou Riser*, violence is also the means by which Prix and the Kaylor sisters are transformed. The nature of violence is to both contaminate and transform the violent. The Kaylor sisters are transformed from executioners (which, I argue, was their original intent) to a tribunal. They are the Furies who become the Eumenides after the "trial" of Riser. For Prix, it is the return of the cycle of violence (being beaten by Comet's daughter) that helps her transform from O.G. to a daughter (to her mother) and friend (to Angel).

In *Come Down Burning*, there is less violence and more pain. While the tale of Skoolie's fall from the tree is shocking in a painful way, it is not violent. Even Tee's death is not violent; there are copious amounts of blood, but it can draw a more sympathetic response than the blood that is let in *Breath, Boom* or *Lou Riser.*

The combination of both retold violence and staged violence could function to further numb an audience already immune to violent images. We are aware, as an audience, that both acts are staged. But there is a difference between the violence portrayed on the screen and that created on stage. On film or video, we know that there are stunt doubles and other methods to create the illusion of violence and its results. On stage we are dealing with live actors in the immediate—real human beings we can reach out and touch. We are aware on some level that what we are watching is illusion, and that the actors are trained in stage combat. The guns cannot be real, or at least they do not have real bullets. But what if there is a mistake? What if the actor playing Anj *really* hits the actor playing Lou, or the actor playing Jupiter really hits the actor playing Prix? What if the actor playing Cat slips from the edge of the bunk bed and actually falls? Our intellectual understanding of live performance provides us with the knowledge that sometimes, mistakes do happen, and at any point, something can go "wrong." There is yet another level, though; we are present, as an audience, at these acts of violence. They are being perpetrated right in front of us. While we go into a theatre for a performance with a willing suspension of disbelief, there is a physical reaction to watching certain acts; our bodies respond in spite of our intellectual understanding. The gun and knife are not as threatening as they might be, because we are aware that there is a long tradition of stage weapons that are not real. However, the hanging of a live human actor on stage is different. The illusion, when well done, is a little too real. We see the actor hanging by the neck, and our physical response is to cringe. We understand that it is not real, but that understanding, that willing suspension, requires an intellectual step back from the world of the play. We must remind ourselves that it cannot be real, in order to reduce our physical response (gasping, tension, increased adrenaline levels, etc.).

Before we can remind ourselves that it is only an illusion, however, we do react. Our bodies' responses bring us closer to the act of murder than the majority of us come in our lifetimes. Because we are a live audience watching live actors, we share in the experience of anxiety, much as we share in the experiences of joy, laughter, and sadness (or even fits of coughing) with our fellow audience members. If we, as the audience, agreed with the sisters' actions up to this point, we are placed in a situation where it is more difficult to agree with their action. In the case of *Lou Riser*, we must ask ourselves if we really believe that death is the appropriate punishment for Riser's crime; by implication, we must also ask ourselves when is death an appropriate punishment for any crime. In *Breath, Boom,* we are implicated in the suicide of Cat, and wonder about what kinds of circumstances create a person (Prix) who could encourage such an act. We must also contend with the issue of gangs and what they offer to young women whose lives have already been filled with violence, and how they contribute both to their survival and their demise. We must face the fact that abortions done by women who have no other choice but to attempt an abortion themselves (or face abortions by untrained people) often result in the death of the woman; we are also made aware that there are circumstances in which abortion is necessary.

Corthron began engaging the issues of violence, racial injustice, and gender in her early plays; her work since has continued to engage these issues. Her plays startle and challenge their audiences through staged and retold violence. They ask us as the audience to reconsider our ideas about the progress of gender issues and race relations in the late twentieth century.

6 Signifying Black Lesbians: Dramatic Speculations

> The history of African American lesbians and gays currently
> exists in fragments, in scattered documents, in fiction, poetry,
> and blues lyrics, in hearsay, in innuendo.
>
> —Barbara Smith (1999: 83)

From work like Yvonne Welbon's documentary *Living With Pride: Ruth Ellis @ 100* to Christa Schwartz's *Gay Voices of the Harlem Renaissance*, black lesbian and gay history has begun to emerge in academic work and in film. As Mattie Udora Richardson demonstrates, "variant sexualities and genders are the things always present in Black history by virtue of their constant disavowal" (64). The histories of black lesbians and gay men lie in the silences and gaps in black history. Representations of black lesbians and gay men are seldom visible in the traditions of black dramatic literature and performance. Those that do exist are often "speculative fiction." By "speculative fiction" I refer to Julie Dash's concept; she "uses the term *speculative fiction* to describe how she would like artists to depict in an 'expansive' way a historical life or period of time about which historical data is lacking" (Erhart 117–18). Though these representations are not abundant, a body of works that represents the lives of black lesbian/queer/same-gender-loving people, both in history and in contemporary U.S. society, is beginning to build.[1]

Historical data for black lesbian life, on which creative artists might base their works, is relatively new. Though recent efforts by historians have begun to uncover a black lesbian history, the amount of scholarship is significantly smaller than the histories of white lesbians and gay men and white queer communities. My effort here is to use "speculative fictions" of black lesbian life—specifically, two dramatic texts—to examine the ways in which "black lesbian" is signified in the various communities in which black lesbians live. A close analysis of *A Lady and a Woman* and *blood pudding*, two contemporary plays by and about black lesbians, invokes a "speculative fiction" about black lesbian life. This "fiction" can lead us to a deeper understanding of and appreciation for the complexity of black lesbian culture and history as it has existed and continues to exist in often precarious relationships to the culture and life of "America."

I should make clear, however, that in examining these speculative fictions of black lesbian life, I am not seeking to provide a final, "correct," or "true" representation. Rather, I am interested in the ways in which the characters these two playwrights create reveal the sign systems in use in black queer communities, and how they differ from those used in other communities (broader lesbian, broader African American). The two plays I analyze in depth here, *A Lady and A Woman* by Shirlene Holmes, and *blood pudding* by Sharon Bridgforth, allow me to detail aspects of black lesbian community as it involves complex sets of relationships between and among black lesbian experiences, including butch-femme identities, the complex relationships of gender roles, racial stereotypes, class status, and power.

I begin with a review of representations of black lesbians, and how those representations have been gradually changing over the last thirty years. I consider how the scarcity of these representations creates a scarcity of support for queer women in black communities, and how the issue of homosexuality often thwarts efforts to fight racism. Next, I offer an analysis of *A Lady and a Woman* and *blood pudding*. In the analysis, I feature the constructions of the connections between women, and how these connections reflect the development of "community" that simultaneously transgresses and adheres to core elements of the more widely known "black community." Next, I move to a discussion of the significations and significances of butch and femme in black lesbian life. This discussion is important because butch-femme "roles" reflect yet another level of transgression and adherence between and among black women and the black community, and the black community and the "American" community. Both plays allow us to understand how the butch-femme "roles" are both used and transcended. Finally, I conclude with a brief discussion of "history" in an effort to envision a black lesbian history that creates a broader space within black and "American" culture for the existence of black lesbians. It is a space that is also sufficiently open for a variety of representations to emerge and change without an old and counterproductive battle over what is "authentically" black or lesbian.

Inclusion and Exclusion: Evoking the Black Lesbian

Representations of sexual relationships between women that include women of color are still, unfortunately, fairly scarce. Largely absent in black dramatic literature until the 1960s, there remain few black lesbian characters even in contemporary drama. Among those, Cheryl West's Vennie in *Jar the Floor* is probably the most familiar to theatre audiences, because

West's 1991 play is still produced in regional theatres. Most plays featuring black lesbian characters are plays by black lesbians; they are notably absent from most anthologies and are typically produced at small theatres that specialize in black queer works, like the company A Real Read, in residence at Bailiwick Repertory Theatre in Chicago.

Ed Bullins is one of the playwrights of the Black Arts Movement of the 1960s and continues to be known for his dramatic examinations of working-class blacks. In 1965, he wrote a play called *Clara's Ole Man,* in which a young man named Jack, evidently oblivious to the signs, attempts to arrange a date with Clara. Clara had told him that her "old man" worked in the afternoon, so he has come over with the intention of spending some time with Clara. When he arrives, however, he discovers that Big Girl, Clara's "old man," has stayed home from work. Big Girl plays the masculine (butch) role within their relationship; she works and is the family breadwinner and in behavior takes the role of the gendered male. She drinks with Jack and teases him until the nature of her relationship with Clara is revealed. When Jack responds by retching, Big Girl has him beaten up by some neighborhood thugs. That Bullins would write such a play in the mid 1960s, painting Jack as an obvious fool, is a testament to the undercurrent of nominal acceptance of the black lesbian within her own community, within certain class strictures. Acceptance is much more likely in working-class communities than in middle or upper middle class ones; "though lesbians and gay men were exotic subjects of curiosity, they were accepted as part of the community (neighborhood)—or, at least, there were no manifestos calling for their exclusion from the community" (Clarke 41). The presence of Big Girl in black dramatic literature does not necessarily mean, however, that her representation is seen as positive. Both Jewell Gomez and Cheryl Clarke mention this play specifically when critiquing representations of black lesbians. For Gomez, the play "fed into the established stereotypes I'd expected" (Gomez 169). The characterization of Big Girl was, for Gomez, one-dimensional, controlling, and rude. She argues that "Bullins trotted out the very antilesbian rhetoric that has pervaded middle-class black life" (170). Cheryl Clarke is even stronger in her discussion of the play, which she calls "another classic example of sixties-style black woman hatred" (Clarke 36). While she notes that Clara and Big Girl are "not disparaged by their "ghetto" community," this does not save the play from being, in her view, "a substanceless rendering of the poor black community, a caricature of lesbianism, and a perpetuation of the stereotype of the pathological black community" (37).

Support for the queer woman in black communities has been contingent and nominal. This is not to say that black communities are any more homophobic than any other community; it is, however, to acknowledge that acceptance is a tenuous thing. Recent examples of sexist homophobia (in this instance, homophobia directed specifically at lesbians) within black communities include the assault and murder of Sakia Gunn, a young black lesbian, at a bus stop in New Jersey in May 2003 (Smothers 8). Gunn and several friends were waiting at a bus stop when they were approached by two men in a car. The men asked them if they "wanted some fun"; when they responded that they were gay, the men began to attack them. One of the men stabbed Sakia, killing her.

Homophobic sentiments often emerge from within the black church; the position of the black Baptist and AME churches, as well as the Nation of Islam, is that homosexuality is sinful. Largely, adherence to conservative interpretations of particular Old Testament books ostracizes the black homosexual (male or female) from black churches. Usually, ministers cite the destruction of Sodom and Gomorrah and a passage from Leviticus to bolster their claims of the sinfulness of homosexuality.

In contemporary urban youth (hip hop) culture, however, there is an increasing acceptance of black queer women. The January 2003 issue of *Vibe* included an article on "Aggressives," young urban black women who occupy a queer/transgender space; they "dress and act like males and are attracted to femmes, that is, girlish girls" (Dobie 104). That black queer women could occupy a space in a black popular culture magazine like *Vibe*, and be portrayed positively, is an acknowledgement of the presence of black queer women within black communities. Since then, a few other articles about "AGs" have appeared in the black popular press.

The exclusions experienced by black queer/SGL peoples emerge from the fact of their minority status in the social groups to which they belong, the larger lesbian/gay/bisexual/transgender "community" and the black "community."[2] The issues of the larger lesbian and gay political movements are narrowly constructed as those that are specific to gay identity, which is defined as white and middle class. Even *The Lesbian and Gay Studies Reader*, a classic text in gay/lesbian/queer studies, "displays the consistently exclusionary practices of lesbian and gay studies in general" (Hammonds 127). Therefore, issues that are important to queer people of color (like racism) are not considered "gay enough" to be part of the larger agenda.

On the other hand, some Afrocentric scholars claim that homosexuality is a European invention, and that same-sex relationships are not appropriate, and in fact are dangerous to African diaspora peoples.[3] This claim denies scholarship relating specifically to the broad spectrum of same-sex relationships that have appeared in a variety of African cultures.[4]

Shirlene Holmes's *A Lady and a Woman* and Sharon Bridgforth's *blood pudding* are relatively contemporary plays that mark the movement toward opening a space for representing black lesbians on stage. These plays address the "silence, erasure, and invisibility" that have plagued representations of black women's sexual lives (Hammonds 130). Both of these plays place their black lesbian couple within black communities; as a result, they have no connection or physical proximity to white lesbian communities. The two plays are stylistically very different. Holmes's work is a realistic play about the development of an intimate sexual relationship between two black women, placed in the context of a black community and its struggle for existence in the late nineteenth century. Bridgforth's play is a nontraditional poetic drama in which we come to see how the experiences of the characters are emblematic of an entire community and that community's history. Both plays take place in the South, where the playwrights are able to evoke communities that are more or less exclusively black, and that have strong black working-class cultures.

Love: Black Lesbian Verisimilitude

Shirlene Holmes's *A Lady and a Woman* creates representations of love and desire between black women; Holmes's Biddie and Flora make their love work in a late-nineteenth-century African American community. Flora, who owns an inn, meets Biddie when Biddie comes to town, looking for a room. Flora has one available, and she offers it to Biddie. The play centers on the development of the relationship between the women; they grow closer until their relationship becomes sexual. While they deal with jealousy and denial, the two maintain a good relationship and eventually adopt an unwanted child.

The first scene of the play establishes the common ground on which they stand as two single women. The playful banter between them begins in that first scene, establishing a mutuality that might have been unlikely, considering the different social locations of the two women. The differences between them are those that Holmes constructs in the title of her play: while Flora is a "lady," Biddie is a "woman." Their difference is more than one of semantics, but the difference between words that signify gender in different ways; "lady" evokes a different kind of femininity than "woman." Holmes introduces the characters as embodying different kinds of womanness, the difference between two *lesbian* genders (as opposed to "man" and "woman," the gender possibilities in a heteronormative culture).

The subtle flirtation between Flora and Biddie begins in the first scene of the play. The conversation that introduces them to each other establishes Biddie as a tenant in Flora's rooming house. It only takes a few days for

Flora and Biddie to connect emotionally. Biddie sees in Flora a potential mate: she is a "good sight to come home to," and would "make a man a good wife" (190). Flora shies away repeatedly. There are moments when she plays along with Biddie, when she connects with her on an emotional level, but it takes a little longer for her to move from emotional to physical. She is unsure, having never had a woman lover, whether this is right. She understands that it feels right, but she worries about it all the same.

It takes a month in the time of the play for Flora to move the friendship between herself and Biddie to love. It is not a simple transformation; the development of her relationship with Biddie is complex and requires a transformation of Flora's self-concept. She mentions after she and Biddie have spent their first night together, "I've had women friends for as long as I been in this world and never once laid hands on them. I always knew that wasn't right. But here you come and it seem like I'm supposed to" (198). Flora has never allowed herself to have sexual feelings for other women, but Biddie's presence and persistence give her the opportunity. Of course, nothing would have happened if Flora had not already had the emotional connection to Biddie that she did and the willingness to make the connection physical as well.

Holmes gives the love story between Flora and Biddie a happy ending; they stay in their community and adopt an unwanted child. Their relationship is not idealized; like most couples, they have their arguments and deal with jealousy. It also defies the very negative stereotypes of the sexuality of black women that black women playwrights have long avoided. They are not promiscuous, nor are they obsessed with sex; they do not embody the "*promiscuity* or excessive or unrestrained heterosexual desire" or the "unrestrained homosexual desire" of the stereotype of black female sexuality (Collins 97). They form a monogamous, long-term relationship, attend church, and otherwise go about their lives in the same ways that their neighbors do. Their taking-in of an unwanted child underscores another important function of lesbians in earlier African American communities: the women who took in unwanted children, whether related to them or not, helped to maintain community and culture. In fact, results of the 2000 census estimate that some 61 percent of black lesbian couples raise children (Swarns 24).

Flora and Biddie do not live in a "lesbian" community. Their community is their larger community, a small southern black town within which each performs vital roles. The community that Holmes represents in her play is one in which women who choose to create lifelong partnerships and families with other women are just another kind of family. It is idealistic to believe that such a relationship would not draw comment or condemnation from some within this larger community. However, as speculative fiction, Holmes is free to create a community in which homosexual relationships would exist side by side with heterosexual relationships. The fiction re-encounters reality when Flora uses the term "bulldagger," well-known as a disrespectful term for lesbian (specifically butch), for it is clear that the term is a negative (or dismissive) one that is used to reference Biddy by others in town.

Sharon Bridgforth's play *blood pudding* is based on her poetic novel *the bull-jean stories*, which won a Lambda Literary Award in 1998. She creates an imagined history of a southern (particularly New Orleans) black community through her character bull-jean, the black lesbian "folk-hero." Bridgforth's play combines ritual, festival, and poetic form; in its interdisciplinarity, it interrogates various constructions—history and contemporary representations of bodies, identities, and sexualities. It demonstrates the deep connection of black lesbians to black communities, history, and cultures; it also constructs an image of love and desire between black women.

Bridgforth has the ability to create character and to write history through lyrical, poetic "monologues." The characters/speakers emerge as individuals relating stories. These stories tell the history of the people of a region, while they also tell a history of the women loving women who have been, and remain, an important part of many black communities. One of the most important things that this work does is to give voice to members of the black community who are visible but invisible, who are considered marginal but are central to so many lives and stories. While the stories are ostensibly about bull-jean, they are really about a whole community of women.

Bridgforth sets the stage in a scene that evokes the sounds of black Creole New Orleans:

> Play low down red light piano blues/in places red light
>   don't mean stop it mean
> Come on in/my daddy
> Make that piano moan
> Make it holla to heaven
> rock out of sight
> my daddy taught me how to play (9)

The piano player is "Docta Gombo"; she has her own style: "alila mam'ma—alila daddy—some warrior—some slave—and the drum" (9).

The place where Docta Gombo plays piano is the "club seeyaround," where black Creoles spent time from "late Friday till mid-Sunday," and where we first encounter bull-jean. Most of the stories are about bull-jean, although they are not told by her. As Robert Faires wrote in the *Austin Chronicle*, "the story flows forth like water, bubbling, cascading over time and place, swirling us through this time and that, there and here, sometimes in the sound of one voice, sometimes in the sound of many. As always, Bridgforth's sensibility is fluid, shifting setting and perspective, giving us one point of view, then another, until we find ourselves surrounded by the various currents of narrative and history" (Faires).

The stories of bull-jean and her community of women-loving-women emerge. bull-jean, serafine, big brigette, red lily, tufus, papa ann, read, babet, and mina form a community that sits within the larger black community but is not separate from it. In other words, what they form is not an explicit lesbian community in the way we would think about lesbian community today. Rather, they live, work, play, and love with a degree of acceptance in the larger black community. This may be one of the most radical things about Bridgforth's script: she gives voice and history to a black lesbian community that has always existed, even if it has not defined itself precisely in that way. When we first encounter bull-jean, she is at club seeyaround, big brigette's place. serafine is singing, casting a spell over the audience:

> bull-jean was there.
> at her table in the corner in the front
> she waited
> like everybody else
> cept bull-jean wasn't gripped on a drank
> like some of us/no
> cause drank
> done already made her dead
> and crazy/well but
> that's a whole nutha story/yeah (10)

serafine's performance creates a disturbance at the club, and big brigette throws tufus, the origin of the problem, out.

> tufus mam'ma was there
> went on out too/madd cause
> tufus donn pause our good-got-damn-day of rest. (12–13)

Club seeyaround is everyone's club; it is not exclusively lesbian or heterosexual space. The club is the primary representation of the inclusivity of the community. Though that inclusivity is not complete, it is significant. This is a community in which sexuality does not determine one's acceptance.

As for bull-jean, we come to understand that the end of her relationship with babet is the cause of her current state. babet refused to be involved with bull-jean as long as bull-jean insisted upon partying with read every weekend, from Friday night until Sunday morning. The loss of babet has made bull-jean give up "her bottle and her bad ackn" (16).

bull-jean is accustomed to having just about any woman she wants, including women who are married to men (although this story is not in *blood pudding*, but is in *the bull-jean stories*, Bridgforth's first poetic novel). Eventually, she settles on mina. mina was raised by her cousin, and it is this cousin who recounts to us the story of the start of mina and bull-jean's relationship. mina has been married before and is not looking to be anyone's wife again. She says:

> why you tryn ta call me yo wife bull-jean
> wife
> what do that mean anyway?
> i been called wife befo
> turned my whole Life ova ta the concept/ta
> obey ta have foever till death   i donn
> that/already died once
> wasting prayers on makbelieve [. . .]
> look like wife
> is a word folk use when they want
> license to control you   if you tryin
> ta claim me bull-jean/jes call me yo wo/mn
> that's what i am
> a wo'mn,
> complete,
> with or without you
> [. . .]
> wife
> ain't saying nuthn right/in my mind! (18–19)

There is a clear distinction for mina between the meaning of "wife" and the process of being in a mutually respectful relationship with another person. Fortunately, what bull-jean wants from mina is someone who will "make this journey / this Life" with her, being true to herself (20). What we know of bull-jean at the end of this scene is that at least for now, she has a happy ending. What emerges from her pursuit of mina is a mutually respectful, loving relationship.

There are ways in which Bridgforth's community, like Holmes's community, is idealistic. bull-jean does eventually find love, but not without trials and tribulations. Like Holmes's play, differences in sexuality are not cause for condemnation or exclusion from the community. Unlike in Holmes's play, however, bull-jean lives in a community of women who love women, even if "lesbian" is not a term they would use to describe themselves. In both plays, we have love relations that develop between women and form "butch/femme" couplings. I turn now to an examination of "butch" and "femme."

Butch and Femme: Black Lesbian Desire

In both *A Lady and a Woman* and *blood pudding*, the primary relationships that develop between women could be classified as "butch" and "femme," with Biddie and bull-jean as the "butch" women and Flora and mina as the "femme" women. The codes of butch and femme identity are not only present in these plays but are in some ways crucial to the constructions of desire in black lesbian communities, particularly those of the past. In this manner both Holmes and Bridgforth inject actual history into their imagined histories. The extent to which butch/femme couplings are part of communities of lesbian culture is evidenced in the writings of many lesbians of color; Cherie Moraga's *Giving Up the Ghost* and Jewell Gomez's *The Gilda Stories* are two such works. "There are a lot of reasons that butch-femme was such a standard way of behavior in the black community, and I think a lot of it has to do with class. People frequently denigrate butch-femme because it was a working-class response to lesbian life" (Findlay 153).

Butch and femme identities have been a topic of investigation and discussion since the 1970s, when emergent lesbian feminists, many of whom were white and middle class, favored abandoning the classic "roles" because they were considered dangerous mimicry of heterosexuality, and that they were "negative and restricting" (Jeffries 160). The explanations of butch and femme embodiment that were common in the 1980s focused on hierarchies (butch above femme), adoption of femme to conform to societal expectations of women, and the reclamation of butch and femme identities as romanticized nostalgia of the 1950s. The early study of a black lesbian community in St. Louis in the mid-1960s by Ethel Sawyer (1965) revealed butch (or "stud") as the identifiable "lesbian" identity, whereas femme ("fish") was a transitional identity between heterosexuality and homosexuality, and homosexuality was signified by the adoption of a "stud" identity. There were those who remained femme, although they were not completely considered lesbian by other "studs."

By the 1990s, however, the academic investigations into butch and femme (as well as other lesbian identities) had reclaimed them not as mimicry of heterosexuality but as lesbian subject positions or as ways of being (in a phenomenological sense). Judith Butler's philosophical musings on gender and gender identity in her article "Performative Acts and Gender Constitution," published in the 1990 anthology *Performing Feminisms: Feminist Critical Theory and Theatre*, triggered a theoretical push in feminist theatre studies to investigate the aspects of play and parody inherent in butch and femme identities.[5] Certainly these theoretical advancements were an improvement over the anti–butch/femme pronouncements of the lesbian feminists of the 1970s and '80s, but I argue that even these contemporary theories do not fully take up the everyday lived experience of women who identify as butch and femme.

Sue-Ellen Case's work on butch and femme as parody and play broke new theoretical ground in feminist theatre studies. She began an exploration of butch/femme in her essay "Towards a Butch-Femme Aesthetic." Case argues that masculinity and femininity are roles that can be taken up and played by anyone, and the idea of butch and femme as "performative" (meaning consciously performed, rather than the preconscious habitual performance in the phenomenological sense) has permeated theatre, performance, and queer studies.

We understand, through both feminist and queer theory, that social, gender, and sexual roles are taken on or learned. They also emerge out of lived experience and the habits of bodily comportment. The lives and experiences of the Aggressives offer us a contemporary example of black lesbian embodiment. They do identify as women, but as Aggressives they are frequently mistaken for men (not that it bothers them). Dobie notes that "all of the Aggressives I meet hate the words 'butch' and 'dyke,' and don't even like 'lesbian' much. They prefer to say simply, 'I'm gay. I like girls'" (Dobie 107). They enjoy a freedom from the meanings and negative significations of "butch," "dyke," or "lesbian," as well as the association of those terms with white women. Sherrie Inness's study of butchness reveals that "being butch is more complicated than merely slipping on a man's suit and tie; it also entails adopting behavioral patterns that are typically perceived as nonfeminine" (186). Carriage and demeanor are essential elements of her "masculine" image because they are the *embodiment* of butchness. Following Inness, I argue here, with both Holmes and Bridgforth's characters as part of my evidence, that where the "role" ends and the human begins is much more than putting on a costume or adhering to a social stereotype. Reflective of contemporary and historic evidence from some communities, both Bridgforth and Holmes's lesbians/communities are not places where butch is the only legitimate lesbian identity. Although Inness would argue that the reliance on a butch/femme coupling in *A Lady and a Woman* reinforces the idea that butch/femme is the only possible lesbian coupling, it is more historically accurate to the period. *blood pudding* is much less concerned with the butchness or femmeness of any characters other than bull-jean. Judith Halberstam's work calls butchness "female masculinity" and engages race specifically as an element of female masculinity. Halberstam is interested in the different kinds of masculinity, particularly as those masculinities intersect with race and class. Her analysis of both the role of Cleo in *Set It Off* (1996) and contemporary black drag kings also contributes to the understanding of the complexities of black masculinities and femininities.

Engaging Butch/Femme Desire and Identity

Both Holmes's and Bridgforth's plays feature a couple we could describe as butch/femme. One of the first ways we distinguish between the "lady" and the "woman" of Holmes's play is visually—by their attire when we first encounter them on the stage. This is typically the way that one identifies butch or femme, because clothing is a primary signifier of gender identity. Flora is busy running her inn, dressed in a "rather low cut dark purple cotton handmade dress" (186). Biddie, on the other hand, is "a mannish . . . butcher wearing a leather hat, vest, and pants" (186). What is immediately apparent from the way that Holmes describes the women is that their professions are part of how they present themselves. Flora runs an inn, and Biddie is a butcher. Biddie's work is not traditionally female, and she does not present herself as traditionally female. Her masculinity, as Inness would argue, "is the chief identifying trait of the butch" (Holmes 203). She does not embody "lady" in the way that Flora does. When Flora questions her about it, she explains, "I was the only girl in a house of ten brothers. And the oldest, too, so I spent lots of time doing hard work. Every time I tell my daddy that my back was hurting from the lifting and picking and carrying three and five times my weight, he'd spit and say, 'Gal, you din't got no back. All you got is gristle'" (188–89). In other words, Biddie has acquired her masculine embodiment through her long years of hard work typically done by men. It is unlikely that Biddie would have an identifiably "feminine" body comportment after the years she has spent doing physical labor. Biddie also tries to make the difference between them obvious to Flora. When Flora tries to call her "miss," Biddie explains that she is woman, not a lady: "You're the flower. I'm the blade. You seal up and I open up. You the kind that carries and I'm the kind that hauls"; the difference between carrying and hauling is analogous to the difference between Biddie and Flora, between butch and femme (189). Biddie's butchness emerges from her everyday life, as Flora's femmeness emerges from hers.

While the butch and femme identities emerge clearly in the written scripts, in performance it is necessary to physically represent the butch and femme identities to the audience. The "butch" and "femme" identities must be readable to the audience; this can be somewhat tricky, depending on the audience. Black women are typically viewed as less feminine by white culture, the lines between butch and femme in the black community are specific to it, and the signs that differentiate between the two gender positions do not always correspond to those for white lesbian culture. As Patricia Hill Collins explains, "the stereotype of women athletes as 'manly' and as being lesbians and for Black women as being more 'masculine' than

White women converge to provide a very different interpretive context for Black female athletes" (135). Because of the idea that black women are more masculine, black female athletes who are heterosexual highlight their heterosexuality in order to be seen as heterosexual in spite of their physical strength. Black women are identified as more "masculine" than white women, even though they are heterosexual; a black woman embodying what we might call "black femininity" is understood to be heterosexual. We might, through Collins's discussion of black female athletes, investigate what signifies "black femininity."

Seldom have black female athletes competed in sports that are considered traditionally "feminine," like figure skating and gymnastics. Both figure skating and gymnastics emphasize grace, delicacy, and notions of white femininity. As Abigail Feder notes briefly, black women have usually been thought "too athletic" to be successful in the artistic elements of figure skating. Feder explains that even when black women have competed relatively successfully in figure skating, commentary about their performances has focused on their apparent lack of femininity. Debi Thomas wore a sequined body stocking, rather than a "dress," for her performance in the 1988 Olympics; "although she skated her program 'flawlessly,' according to a Canadian magazine (which might be expected to be free from U.S. partisanship), she received low artistic impression marks," and won the bronze medal; Katarina Witt, whose costume "made her look 'like a member of the Rockette's chorus line,'" won the gold medal (65). Surya Bonaly's warm-up backflip during the 1992 Olympics was regarded as "intimidating" to the sweet and feminine Midori Ito, and U.S. commentary about Bonaly always emphasized her lack of grace and her athleticism. Black women have typically excelled in sports in which their "femininity" is not evaluated in their performance, like track and field events, basketball, and to a lesser degree, softball. Black women who have been successful in sports or other professions that require "femininity" usually conform in some ways to the notions of white "femininity" such as long hair, lighter skin, and small/thin (nonmuscular) body types. In the dominant culture, therefore, in order for black woman to be read as "lesbian," her "masculinity" has to be overdetermined.

Short hair, which is more likely to signify "lesbian" among racial or ethnic groups with very straight hair, does not necessarily signify "lesbian" for black women. A very short, neatly cut natural can be very "feminine" and need not signify "lesbian." Likewise, other natural styles (like locs) are worn by black women of all sexual orientations. Hair style is not necessarily a signifier of lesbian identity among black women; attire and physical comportment are better indicators of the possibility of lesbian identity.

The simplest way to convey butch and femme to an audience (particularly a mixed audience) is to have Flora have longer or straightened hair (or both), and for Biddie to have a very short afro. However, a Biddie in braids or cornrows could be acceptable as butch, as long as her bodily comportment is "masculine." Similar codes hold true for *blood pudding* as well; clearly, bull-jean should convey butch primarily though her bodily comportment, but also through dress and hair. For the other women, particularly as some of those roles are doubled, clothing and comportment will be the primary ways in which butch and femme are signified.

Though Biddie exists in a "masculine" world, that is, a world of work traditionally done by men, she is continually conscious that she is a woman, even while she desires women. Her dress is not an appropriation of the masculine—it is masculine, just as her work is. It would be unsuitable for her to wear "women's" clothing because it would get in the way of her work. Flora, on the other hand, wears the clothing most suited to her work. Holmes also confronts the notion that butch is the only identifiable or legitimate lesbian gender. In other words, one does not have to be butch in order to be a lesbian; one can be femme and lesbian. When Biddie and Flora argue over a woman whom Biddie thinks is interested in Flora, Flora denies the possibility because of the way she looks; in other words, Flora presumes that femininity necessitates a heterosexual identity. Flora says to Biddie, "I can tell you she don't want no woman," and Biddie responds, "You don't know. You didn't want no woman, remember?" (213). Biddie recognized same-sex desire in Flora and is able to recognize it in Linda Ruby as well. Flora worries that people will call her "bulldagger," as they do Biddie, but Biddie assures her that "bulldagger" is not an identity that applies to her. As a femme, Flora is still a "lady," even though she is involved with another woman. "Bulldagger" is a label that attaches only to butchness.

In *blood pudding*, constructions of butch and femme identity are more complex. bull-jean, as the central character of the work, occupies a position that allows her and other butches in the community to exist in a way that is essentially masculine. In other words, the behaviors of bull-jean and other butch women are analogous to the behaviors of men, particularly in their pursuits of other women and weekend partying. Their adoption of masculine behaviors and masculine embodiment, like that of Biddie, is what defines them as butch. As Bridgforth deftly shows us, however, the lasting relationship emerges not out of typical "dog" behavior (bull-dog-jean) she exhibited with babet, but rather through bull-jean's transformation into the equal partner of mina.

The femme women of *blood pudding* are not as strongly developed as characters as bull-jean is. In spite of this, femme identity in bull-jean's community is a complex one. Bridgforth's femmes are as eclectic as those of any contemporary lesbian community. Sexual identity is fluid, and much of that fluidity exists among the femme women in the community. They are not all bisexual, but the majority have had some sexual relationships with men; even bull-jean has had a child. Bridgforth does not rely on descriptions of attire or profession to explain butch or femme; rather, butch and femme as identities emerge out of broader social contexts. For example, Bridgforth describes serafine in the following passage:

> her don't jes walk out
> she appear
> wavy black-brown/thick-hipped/curvy tasty/fiiine
> chocolate
> [...]
> feet-da dadada da hips-swish swish dip and swirl (11)

The words Bridgforth uses to describe serafine's movements, like thick-hipped and curvy, and the description of her hip movement as "swish," "dip," and "swirl," evoke images of movement we typically think of as feminine and are ways that are typically used to describe feminine, as opposed to masculine, comportment.

The implications of femme existence, femme desire, and femme identity are deep, for in every way the lesbian who does not "look like one" transgresses the expectations of the woman who is seen to be heterosexual. While appearing to fulfill the patriarchal notion of femininity, the femme denies patriarchal power over her in part by acting on her desire for women. Key here is the notion of her action, for not only does she, as Case describes, aim her desire at another woman (usually a butch), but she acts on that desire. In the examples cited here, the femme takes an active role in the physical relationship between herself and her woman. Her existence is transgressive by its very nature, even as she is invisible.

Transgression and Adherence: Butch and Femme in Black Communities

Lesbian visibility has largely been the visibility of the butch, who is seen because she does not embody the cultural standard female position. In this, the butch identity is transgressive; it defies the cultural construction of "woman" in dress, manner, work, and so forth. Within black communities, lesbians may be visually identified as transgressive and therefore "butch," but the transgression itself is rendered invisible or ignored. As Beverly Greene states, "some women may find support for their [lesbian] relationship within the African American community or within their families: this support, however, often depends on the maintenance of the invisibility of their relationship" (246). The other way in which black lesbians are rendered invisible is the denial of their identity. This is particularly pertinent for the femme or the woman who does not embody the icon "bulldyke." The codes that the black lesbian embodies are only recognizable as such when she embodies a visible difference, that is, she transgresses the "normative" codes for black women. For the femme, who tends to adhere to the "normative" codes for black women, her lived-body experience is not even necessarily visible when she is actively demonstrating her sexuality. The femme is not a lesbian even though she is walking down the street arm in arm with a "known" lesbian. This is evident both in film and theatre, where the predominant representation of lesbian is of butch. For example, in Bullins's *Clara's Ole Man,* Clara (as a femme) is identified by Jack as a potential sexual partner (i.e., heterosexual) and is not, therefore, a "real" lesbian. In mainstream films, from *Bound* (1996) to *The L Word* (2003), femmes are frequently portrayed as bisexual rather than as lesbian.

The femme, in what appears to be adherence to the cultural construction of "woman," frequently passes for a heterosexual woman, or is passed by a viewer as a heterosexual woman. Though racial passing is usually a conscious choice, the femmes of *blood pudding* and *A Lady and a Woman* never attempt to deceive their "audience" (here, the rest of their community). Rather, their passing is inadvertent: "lesbians who do no look stereotypically 'butch' are more likely to be *forced* to pass [or passed by history] because they lack the masculine attributes that are assumed by most heterosexuals to reveal lesbianism" (italics mine) (Inness 177). Jewell Gomez remarks that "when the three people in that black bookstore dismissed equal rights for gays, they didn't picture me or any of the characters created by Audre Lorde or Cheryl Dunye. They imagined the caricature of lesbians that is repeatedly reinforced by popular culture in films like *Set It Off*" (175).[6] Although the butch is marked in terms of gender and race, the femme is unmarked in her sexuality. In other words, her individual "performance" appears to be normative, insofar as heterosexuality is normative. But, as Peggy Phelan notes, "It is easy to pass as heterosexual because heterosexuality is assumed. In other words, what is made visible is the unmarked nature of heterosexual identity. The one who passes then does not 'erase' the mark of difference, rather the passer highlights the invisibility of the mark of the Same" (Phelan 96).

While Phelan is critical of those who choose to pass as straight, she does not engage the possibility that some lesbians pass because there is a lesbian code of marked and unmarked as well. The unmarked lesbian is the butch; she functions as the visible lesbian both in lesbian culture and in the larger culture. In heterosexual culture, she is marked as lesbian, but in that marking she becomes unmarked; she becomes the "normative" lesbian.

The femme, on the other hand, is consciously the marked "other" in the lesbian community (even, I think, as she is desired as "other"), because she is assumed to be the marked woman/unmarked heterosexual woman in the larger community.

Varying Structures

Holmes and Bridgforth use very different styles and genres. Each has its appeal; because black feminist aesthetics leaves room for the many avenues to artistic expression, they both manifest different aspects of black feminist aesthetics.

Holmes's play is firmly in the tradition of realism in American theatre. It is a single set, although simplified; it can be performed with a minimal set. Holmes's dialogue is also naturalistic; Biddie and Flora speak in sentences as though they are in conversation with each other. By making the artistic vehicle simple, Holmes allows the audience to focus on the character development. Her characters allow the audience to identify with them and to connect with them in intimate ways. Because Holmes is telling a story about these two women, it is important that the audience has easy access to the dialogue of the characters, to their growing relationship, and to them as people. Realism as a form tends to facilitate this kind of connection with the audience.

This is not to say that Holmes's play does not have a political focus; it most certainly does. However, it is possible to create political consciousness through realism. It has also been in the tradition of black feminist playwrights to write realistic dramas in order to bring the audience more intimately into the reality of the lives about which they are writing. When Georgia Douglas Johnson wrote *A Sunday Morning in the South,* she might have written an expressionist play about lynching. The clarity available to her by using realism made it possible for her political point to be located in the situation dramatized. Similarly, the political point of Holmes's play is in the situation she dramatizes: black women do fall in love with each other, make lives together, live various gender expressions, and are important parts of black communities.

Bridgforth draws on a different tradition within black feminist playwrighting, one that connects with the griot, ritual performance, jazz forms, and poetry. Bridgforth creates a loose narrative structure for the play. There is a sense of scenes, although Bridgforth resists constructing formal scenes that have a marked beginning and ending *within the script.* This is not, of course, to say that there are no such divisions. There are about fifteen stories (some not directly related to bull-jean, but most about her and her community) that make up the script. The transitions shift by performer

Fig. 6. Florinda Bryant, Zell Miller, Stacey Robinson, Renita Martin, and Djola Branner in *blood pudding,* Frontera@ Hyde Park, 1998. Photo by Bret Brookshire.

like solos in a live jazz performance; when one story is finished, another begins, like the folks on the front steps of the store in Zora Neale Hurston's Eatonville. By the end of the play, we have a sense not only that we know bull-jean and her community, we have watched her move from forlorn to a woman in love. We also understand the importance of community, of the old folks and the ancestors.

The number of cast members may vary depending on the director's preference. The script has only three necessary "characters" in the cast: a Black Creole (or at least someone who knows enough about black Creole culture to "pass"), bull-jean (the central character around whom the stories in the play coalesce), and the character to which I refer as "the daughter of the Wind," who maintains the ritual format and space of the play. The ritual space is specified in the notes to the play; Bridgforth specifies, "the performance space is an environment that helps to tell the story/intensely inform on a sensory level. The performers should never leave the stage. The set is an Altar" (4). This is essential, because the worlds of the living and the spirit merge at the end of the play. The space becomes literally a ritual space, emerging out of the characters and stories of the play. In her notes to the play, Bridgforth says that this is an Oya work, and that the wind people should be felt. Oya is the Yoruba orisha of sudden change, symbolized by the wind. She is also the only female orisha who is explicitly a warrior. As orisha of the marketplace, Oya represents changes in fortune, from bad to good. As the tornado, she practices selective destruction.[7]

Bridgforth works with and through this figure in the play. In placing bull-jean in the world of Oya, she is in a space where permanence in relationships is hard to achieve, although it is ultimately achievable. The sudden change associated with Oya includes her position as the gatekeeper of the cemetery, which marks the change from the world of the living to the world of the dead. For the audience, the ritual space marks an entrance to a world that is liminal, where the possibility of change and growth can be realized. By writing this way, Bridgforth appeals to a different artistic sense in the audience, one that connects with the stories not only through the stories and characters, but also through the performance itself.

Visioning Black Lesbian History

The efforts of these two playwrights have helped to create, or envision, a history of black lesbians that has not existed in the written histories of black women in the United States. As Bridgforth says in an interview in *BGP* (Baltimore Gay Paper), "I started hearing stories about older, black lesbians. Of course they weren't using that word—lesbian—but older women who clearly had lived with women who were clearly their partners for long periods of time and who were an intricate part of the community there. I wanted to celebrate that and I wanted to explore what that world must be like or have been like and how that world paved the way for me." Bridgforth was, as many of us are, "in awe that there were black lesbians who were an integral, active, well-respected, and well-accepted part of the community" (Spencer 52). Richardson cites Gloria T. Hull's publication of the diary of Alice Dunbar Nelson, a poet and playwright of the early twentieth century and a member of the black women's club movement, as another example of the ways in which black women who were or are central to black communities are "passed" by historians. The fact that Nelson and many of her contemporaries who were club women were also romantically and sexually involved with each other could, in fact, provide another example of the importance of black lesbians to the community. Few black playwrights are writing about black lesbian experience, let alone black lesbian experience that is inextricably connected to the larger black community absent intense homophobia. As we have seen in previous chapters, the contemporary black women playwrights whose works are known more broadly in theatre circles, including Suzan-Lori Parks, Kia Corthron, and Dael Orlandersmith, have not written plays about or including black lesbians.

For black lesbian and queer audiences, both of these plays are validating; the dramatic expression of a black lesbian history, real or imagined, corroborates the feeling and knowledge that black queer existence is not new or an importation of "white depravity." Like the performances of lesbian blues singer Gwen Avery, these plays "function as affirmation, healing, and subversion" (Johnson 94). The meaningful relationship between Biddie and Flora inspires contemporary black lesbian couples by its example of the possibility that one might both be a lesbian and be a "real" member of a black community. Both plays inspire audience response as they re-create situations that are familiar and act as double-entendres (particularly in the case of *A Lady and a Woman*) that are clearly understood by lesbian audiences but might elude other audiences.

Bridgforth's work, not only here in *blood pudding* but also in her recent works *con flama* and *love/conjure blues,* makes explicit the history of black lesbian presence and acceptance in black communities. Similarly, Holmes creates a dramatic presence of black lesbian life that, as evidenced by oral histories like Welbon's film, did exist. While acceptance has varied, there has always been a queer presence in black communities. The efforts to retain and reveal that history, whether real or imagined, are vitally important to the efforts to create accurate representations of black queer women throughout their history in the United States.

7 A Black Feminist Aesthetic

The playwrights whose works I have explored here have much in common, and much that is different. Together in this context, they allow us to sketch out something we might call a black feminist aesthetic. By "aesthetic" I mean not the "beauty" of a text, but rather the elements of the text or performance that invoke a particular history, politics, or philosophy of a "community" (broadly construed). The elements of the text or performance that comprise the aesthetic may range from structure, to plot, to characters. As I noted in chapter 1, the central questions about such an aesthetic are whether or not the text critiques, shifts, or alters representations from dominant culture stereotype, or creates entirely new representations; whether or not the text is structurally consistent with the goals of the "community"; and a conception about the function of the art.

If there is a *core,* a commonality among these very different women, it is they all, in their own ways, construct and reconstruct history and identity. They incorporate history into their works, ensuring that the histories they tell reveal an otherwise hidden history, a black feminist history that centers women's lives and experiences. They also fully embrace the questions of representation of black women and work to refine and reshape them. Despite the vast differences among them in subject, form, and structure, and the iterations of their feminisms, I argue that taken together, the plays I have analyzed here do demonstrate a black feminist aesthetic.

This twenty-first-century black feminist dramatic aesthetic includes the following elements; no single play need have them all, but plays that work within these elements can be described as feminist. The playwright:

1. Uses incidents in the history of blacks in the United States, the diaspora, and Africa to tell a history that is generally unknown to most people in the United States, black and white;

2. Creates "imagined histories" to fill in the gaps in the histories of black women, particularly black lesbians, gay men, and other black "queers," whose histories have been left out;
3. Directly confronts the racist, sexist images of black women that have been projected by the dominant culture;
4. Also confronts the racist images that describe black men as aggressive and/or as rapists;
5. Reveals the abuse that black women suffer at the hands of men of all races;
6. Demonstrates the ways in which institutional racism affects blacks in their dealings with whites and with other blacks;
7. Emphasizes the importance of reproductive freedom for black women;
8. Incorporates oral folk culture or oral urban culture, depending on the focus of the work;
9. Looks deeply into the lives of young women and the challenges that face them, including gang life and education;
10. Addresses an important audience, whether that audience is black women, black people in general, or everyone.

These ten points, to some degree or other, mark the contemporary dramas by black women that reflect developments in black feminist theory; in fact, they are the dramatic representations of that theory and the realization of the aesthetics embedded in black feminist theory.

Histories, Real and "Imagined"

History remains of vital importance to black feminism and black feminist theory and creative production (fiction, drama, performance, music, film) and continues to emphasize the importance of knowing one's history. Often, these histories have become invisible in the curricula of primary and secondary education. In some places, while schools were still segregated, enterprising black teachers ensured that the histories of blacks were incorporated into the curriculum, often to provide inspiration to black children who otherwise might have little hope of a better future.[1] Though I do not want to idealize segregated schools, it is important to note that much of the oral history that was passed down to black children in the 1940s and 1950s is no longer learned in schools. Despite revisions in history curricula across the country, I repeatedly encounter undergraduate students, both black and white, who know little or nothing about post–Civil War Reconstruction, the Exodus of 1879, the Great Migration, or even the date or significance of *Brown v. Board of Education.*

Among the playwrights whose work I have examined here, the "older generation," represented by Pearl Cleage, Breena Clarke, and Glenda Dickerson, most often examines the unknown or forgotten histories of black people. Each of Cleage's full-length plays either take place during an important historical moment or deal directly with the effects of a historical moment. The Exodus of 1879 is skillfully used in *Flyin' West*. By using an actual historical event, Cleage provides a context in which it is possible to see blacks, and particularly black women, not as victims of slavery but as survivors who work to create and keep themselves free. The Exodus as a response to the end of Reconstruction and the revitalization of violence and repression against blacks is an important moment in history, as are the attempts by white speculators to take advantage of blacks. It also provides a way for Cleage to highlight the intersections of race and gender by setting the racial violence against the domestic violence; she quite literally points to the same origin for both kinds of violence.

The point at which the vibrant artistic output of the Harlem Renaissance meets the harsh realities of the incipient Great Depression, the setting for *Blues for an Alabama Sky* is also an important historical moment, but for very different reasons than the Exodus. This moment in history enables Cleage to capture the social importance of the artistic production of the Renaissance while simultaneously reminding her audience that the Renaissance was dependent upon the patronage of whites, and that the fortunes of black artists rose and fell with those fortunes.[2] This period captures the conflicts between the urban sensibilities of blacks who had lived in New York for more than a generation and the influx of blacks from the rural South, who brought with them conservative views out of step with the majority of Harlemites. Cleage's play enables us to see the possibility in the moment, and then to watch it slip away as Delia and Guy pack their bags for Paris.

The most poignant use of history by Cleage is that in *Bourbon at the Border*, where she shows the long-term effects of blacks' struggles against racism. The effects on Charlie and May reverberate and continue to affect their lives some thirty years after the events. Charlie's struggles with depression are a metaphor for the racial depression of post–Civil Rights Movement blacks, who saw the sacrifices and the promise of the 1950s and 1960s collapse under conservative governments and the development of what Patricia Hill Collins calls "the new racism."[3] Having embraced nonviolence during the 1964 Freedom Summer, Charlie now only sees release from his depression in turning outward, instead of inward, the violence that he experienced and continues to experience. Cleage quotes Amiri Baraka's *Dutchman*, in which Baraka implies that the only way to keep from destroying yourself from the inside, as Charlie Parker did, is to turn the anger and violence toward that place from which it emerges: white America. Unfortunately, the killing of white men does not liberate Charlie from his depression, and black violence continues to turn in on itself, devastating its own community.

Where Cleage uses history by engaging in specific periods, Clarke and Dickerson engage the long history of black women in the United States in a single work. Their use of history recalls the names and histories of influential or otherwise "notorious" black women, merged with the historic representations of black women. They create a kind of history of black womanhood, both real and imagined, where racist icons interact with "race women" and activists. Clarke and Dickerson pose a challenge to young black women to learn the history of their foremothers by including more obscure women (Mother Rebecca Jackson) along with the familiar ones (Sojourner Truth). The importance of the words of early black feminists like Anna Julia Cooper resound through the text, while the vulnerabilities of real women like Dorothy Dandridge are poignant reminders of the difficulty of being black and female in the United States.

The "younger" generation of women playwrights also uses history, but in very different ways. Though they invoke the past, they are more likely to use it as a way of revealing the ways in which things have *not* changed. When Suzan-Lori Parks uses history, as she does in *Venus,* she manipulates that history in order to make a point about representation. By pointing to the icon of "the butt," Parks not only reveals the origin of an icon of black female sexuality, but encourages her audience to think about contemporary implications. The connection made in chapter 2 between Sara Baartman's derriere and Jennifer Lopez's is also made by Patricia Hill Collins. Collins takes that connection one step further when she states:

> It's one thing if Jennifer Lopez and Beyoncé Knowles from Destiny's Child profit from their own images and present themselves in performance as "bootylicious." It's entirely another if adolescent girls tap into this message of female power and head off to their eighth grade classrooms decked in the same "bootylicious" apparel, all the while purchasing the clothes required to achieve this image with money they don't have. The theme here is not censorship of Black girls, but rather to question whether they can "handle it" if they are so woefully uninformed about the legacy of Sarah Bartmann [*sic*]. (50)

The function of imagined histories, of "speculative fictions," fulfills a very different role in black feminist drama. The use of history in these instances (certainly Holmes and Bridgforth, but also Corthron to some degree) is to fill in the unknown history. This history is not unknown because it has been ignored, but rather because it has been lost. These are the histories that are passed down through oral tradition, within families, in family Bibles and gossip. The documentation of these histories—of black lesbians and bisexual women, and of poor rural women—has either not existed physically or has not been kept. These are the histories that do not seem important, because they exist even further on the margins than other black histories and women's histories. These imagined histories, then, fill a gap in history by imagining what has not left a physical record.

Addressing Black Female Identity

The project of reinventing black identity—particularly black female identity—remains one of the key projects in black feminism. For this reason, all of the works examined in this text have taken on, to some degree, the issue of the representation of black female identity. Some of these are critiques of historic stereotypes and icons, while others offer new, "reinvented" images of black female identity to challenge those historic ones.

Of course, the work that most overtly challenges stereotypes of black women is *Re/Membering Aunt Jemima*. All of the aspects of mass media portrayals show up in this play: Aunt Jemima (complete with handkerchief), several aspects of the tragic mulatta, Sapphire, and a Jezebel of sorts, Tiny Desiree. Clarke and Dickerson do not allow these images to stand unchallenged, though. All of these stereotypes undergo a humanizing; doses of reality illuminate the ways in which the icons tell only part of the story. By including Dorothy Dandridge, the real life of a woman cast in film and in life as a tragic mulatta injects a dose of reality. Most important of the images that Dickerson and Clarke reimagine, or "re/member," is that of Aunt Jemima.

If we recover, or reinvent, the image of Aunt Jemima in the image of a black woman who is ill and resists the efforts of white society to ridicule, silence, or kill her, then what was once a racist image of the alleged support of black women for white society now changes. That image is transformed into one that represents the collective strength and resolve of black women, who celebrates her larger body and nappy hair as beautiful, and who comes from a long line of "race women" who have struggled against racism and sexism.

Other reinventions of identity appear in the plays of the "younger" generation as well. Unlike their older colleagues, the younger playwrights have experienced freedom similar to that of their Harlem Renaissance foremothers in that they are able to create representations of black women that are not necessarily positive. In other words, they are freer to represent contemporary black women who live at the painful intersections of race, gender, and class. These include representations like Hester in *In The Blood,* whose five children by different fathers seems to simply replicate a stereotype that black America would prefer to forget, and one that we try to avoid. The argument against using images like Hester is that in a world of limited representations of black women, representations of black women *should* prove our "humanity," our equality with white women, and our desire to "get out of the ghetto." Parks is not afraid to engage with the "negative" images of black women, and in so doing, she works at making visible the ways in which all of society—black and white—is implicated in the existence of women like Hester.

Hester's ignorance is easily matched by the manipulation and disregard for her well-being shown by all of the characters who are supposed to help her—the middle-class black woman (who should understand her struggles), the preacher (who takes advantage of her sexually), and the fathers of her children. Parks indicts these other black characters for their refusal to help Hester; in doing so, she indicts the black middle and upper class for their refusal to help change the circumstances for poor blacks. Her challenge is a poignant echo of Alice Childress's *Wine in the Wilderness,* particularly in the black social worker who replicates the attitudes of white society and the "messed-up chick" who bears the brunt of middle-class blame. In spite of her ignorance, Hester comes across as a sympathetic character; she is where she is because institutional racisms persist.

Similarly, Corthron's Prix, the gang leader, is a "negative" representation in a culture in which blacks and gangs are typically equated in urban environments. Corthron opens the concept of the inner-city black gang by looking at female gang members and the ways in which they are similar to, and different from, male gang members. Prix's violence and her lack of concern for the lives of others (as seen both by her watching Cat commit suicide and by her past violence) would make her unsympathetic if it were not for her fascination with fireworks and the intelligence that fascination suggests. While we may wonder if Prix could have had a different life, we are also sympathetic to the circumstances of her youth: as a witness to violence against her mother and a victim of rape, we do not wonder why Prix has this outlook on life.

In both of these examples, the female characters show us a segment of black life in the United States that is both highly visible and invisible. The black welfare mother or female gang banger are overdetermined stereotypes that suffuse our popular media, from television news to film and music video. In taking up these images, though, both Corthron and Parks do not allow them to simply stand, unexamined; they ask their audiences to question the veracity of the sign they invoke and then deconstruct. For a culture that is deeply connected to its liberalism, the idea that the "playing field" is not level is a deep, substantial critique.

Wrestling with Demons

In addition to their work with history and identity—two critical elements of a black feminist aesthetic—the contemporary black feminist playwright also addresses racism and sexism more explicitly and sometimes separately. While Parks uses her character Hester to critique and deconstruct the icon of the black welfare mother, she also addresses welfare and recent "reforms" to welfare. Welfare is an issue that affects women across races, and white women continue to comprise the majority of welfare recipients. That the welfare recipient has been represented as a black woman with many children whose fathers she does not know is well known. In this play, Parks reveals the conundrum in which many women on welfare now find themselves. Although Hester would like to stay home with her children (a privilege reserved for middle- and upper-class women), she is required by the welfare agency to work. The jobs for which she is trained are insufficient to care for her family of six and do not afford her childcare for her young children who are not in school. She is left living under a bridge, illiterate, until she snaps and kills one of her children.

Environmental justice in the face of poverty is another of the "demons" with which contemporary black feminists wrestle. It is most visible in Corthron's *Splash Hatch on the E Going Down,* where environmental toxins affect the lives of all characters. Thyme is left a widow at seventeen because her young husband contracts lead poisoning from his job. The harsh realities of the labor market for a high school dropout mean that Erry works in a job that his employers know is hazardous. He is not eligible for health insurance until he is so far along in his illness that he does not survive. If he complains, he risks being fired from one of the few jobs that pays a living wage.

Thyme's friend Shaneequa suffers from asthma, which is increasingly common among residents of inner cities.[4] Though the causes of higher rates of asthma vary, Shaneequa's is connected to the environmental toxins she breathes in while she is in the local park, built on top of a landfill. Corthron evokes the resistance of minority communities to increased exposure to environmental toxins, particularly in inner cities, where low attentiveness makes minority communities vulnerable to city plans to locate landfills and incinerators in their neighborhoods.

In addition to environmental concerns and welfare, domestic violence is an issue of great importance to contemporary black feminists, and it appears in several of the plays examined here. Most explicitly, domestic violence is used as a significant plot element in *Flyin' West*. The abuse of black women is constructed as antiblack; in other words, for a black man to beat a black woman is to hurt the project of racial equality. Black men must treat black women with the respect they were not afforded as slaves.

Domestic violence also appears in *Breath, Boom*. In this case, it is a contemporary example, even if the ultimate response is the same (both men are killed). Prix's mother has access to a legal system that is supposed to protect her, one to which Minnie did not have access in 1879. In spite of improvements in the law, Mother does not have a way to keep Jerome from harming her. She has a restraining order, but she has not had the emotional and psychological support that might keep her from allowing him to come into her house. While Min and her "sisters" have a happy ending, Prix's long history of violence, crime, and incarceration come partially as a result of living in a violent household.

Her Body, Her Destiny

African American feminists have long considered having rights over one's own body and sexuality essential. Issues of black women's bodies are abundant in the plays examined here. Abortion is a contentious issue in the history of African Americans. On the one hand, the choice by black women slaves to abort rather than bear children who would become slaves, or who were the result of their rape, was an important one. On the other hand, abortion has at times been considered a practice aimed at genocide. The origin of the birth control movement in the United States was linked to the eugenics movement and was in some quarters strongly resisted. Whether the issue is the right to not breed slaves for white slave masters, or to have children that are wanted, issues of reproductive rights have always been important to black women. Cleage's invocation of the birth control movement in *Blues for an Alabama Sky* connects it to the activism of black women in the Harlem Renaissance who were actively supporting birth control, like playwright Katherine Tillman. Plays that voice concerns about coerced sterilization, or court-ordered long-term birth control, raise additional issues in contemporary reproductive rights.[5] However, the issue of abortion is linked to several others for black women. As we see in Corthron's *Come Down Burning*, abortion is sometimes necessary to ensure the survival of children who are already born. Skoolie pushes Tee to abort her latest pregnancy because there are barely enough resources for the four of them, and they cannot afford to feed another mouth. Similarly, in *Blues for an Alabama Sky*, Cleage argues (through Delia) that family planning is one way to help alleviate poverty and improve families' financial status. Sam performs abortions (in secret, because they are not legal at the time) because he also deems them necessary.

While black feminists maintain the right of women to have abortions, it does not mean that they are not ambivalent about the practice. Angel's abortion precipitates a string of events that culminates in murder. Cleage is critiquing the attitudes embodied by Lester that women should be baby-making machines, but Angel's choice to have an abortion is also tied to her bad choices. The abortions that the Baron performs on Venus are an element of the continued abuse of Venus; they are for his convenience, not hers. She has very little sovereignty over her own body, including when or whether she will become pregnant or bear a child. The issue of sterilization also appears. Hester is told that she is required to have a hysterectomy because she will not stop having children. She remains largely clueless about the procedure or the implications for her life; her "consent" is illegitimate because she is unable to read the consent form. For the most part, the women who we might think would choose abortion do not. Thyme, Hester, Shaneequa, and other women choose to have their children even though that decision makes their lives more difficult.

On issues of sex and sexuality, black feminists are still working against the stereotypes of black women's animalistic, wanton sexuality. That does not mean that sexuality is confined to monogamous relationships or expressed only in innuendo, but it is often expressed there. From Thyme and Erry to Flora and Biddie, many of these plays present monogamous, committed relationships between blacks. This is important because it is still necessary to counter the image perpetuated in mass media that black people are incapable of maintaining traditional nuclear families. These constructions of functional families, when heterosexual, redefine black masculinity as one in which black men are not abusive sexists but rather work with black women against both sexism and racism. The very idea of representing black lesbians in monogamous, committed relationships is not only contemporary but is not likely to be found in any but feminist texts.

These playwrights do not feel restricted to representing only "positive" images, though, and some of the plays use black female sexuality that might seem stereotypical. Their use here is not to titillate or to reinforce the stereotype; rather, their use makes a larger point about U.S. culture and the lives of real black women. Hester is one of the clearest examples of this. Parks creates in Hester a character that has multiple sexual partners and has children by many different men. Her intention is not to perpetuate the idea that the only thing black women on welfare do is have children, which is the myth. Instead, Parks portrays Hester as someone who has no control over her life, and that includes her sexuality. The myth of black female sexuality is used by those around Hester who take advantage of her.

Jemima's many men might also initially seem to revive the stereotype of the black women with many children by different fathers. However, Clarke and Dickerson use the different men with whom Jemima has relationships to highlight the attributes of those children. Whether they are strong or tortured depends on who their fathers were. The mythic mammy is typically represented as asexual, caring only for the white children in her care. Jemima, on the other hand, cares deeply for her children. Her multiple sex partners also remind the audience of the lack of agency that black slave women had over their bodies, their reproduction, and their sexuality.

The openness of the sexuality of a character like bull-jean provides a unique space in the treatment of black female sexuality. bull-jean embodies a confident, self-assured sexuality in which she is in control of her own body and understands her own desire. Bridgforth is not afraid of putting bull-jean—or black female sexuality—on stage. Because her work (not only in *blood pudding* but also in her more recent works *con flama* and *love/conjure blues*) does not attempt to critique previous representations of black female sexuality, Bridgforth does not restrict herself to creating characters whose purpose is to dispel myths (except, perhaps, that black lesbians do not exist).

Young, Black, and Female

Teen pregnancy is an issue of concern to contemporary black feminists, and it also emerges in the body of work studied here. Corthron's interest in the lives of young black women necessitates some treatment of teen pregnancy. Her most unconventional treatment of teen pregnancy is that of Thyme in *Splash Hatch on the E Going Down*. Thyme is not poor and is not illiterate; she comes from a middle-class family and is highly intelligent. The assumption that teenagers become pregnant because they do not know how *not* to is disrupted and, as mentioned in chapter 4, sometimes not credible to the audience. Thyme chooses to have her baby and is married to her child's father, even though they both live with her parents. Thyme's eventual single motherhood is not a result of an irresponsible young black man, but rather the result of a responsible, if not highly intelligent, young black man who dies while trying to provide for his family with less than a high school education. The harsh realities of trying to finish school while pregnant or a mother are highlighted.

Many of the teens in these plays are troubled. Though a number of them struggle with pregnancy and motherhood, others must live with the violence that surrounds them. Most clearly, violence is an issue in *Breath, Boom,* where it is thematic. Corthron searches for the roots of youth violence and finds them in a world/society/community in which violence is endemic. It is not surprising that Prix is violent; the only surprise, perhaps, is that she is female. Corthron's interest in violence, its origins, and its expressions is clearly evident in her early work, particularly in *Wake Up, Lou Riser.* The Kaylor sisters engage in a kind of gang violence when they capture and beat Riser, and Corthron's treatment of their situation excuses their violence because it is ultimately less than the violence that was committed against them.

The pressures and issues of young black women are significantly different than those faced by earlier generations of black women. HIV/AIDS infection is growing fastest among young black women, and prevention education has not been effective in reaching them. The "epidemic" of violence on inner-city streets not only affects young black men but also young black women and girls, who try to survive in whatever ways they can. That often means needing to be part of a gang for protection, even if being part of a gang is dangerous. Chronic illness like asthma steadily increase for black youth, particularly those who live in cities, and changes to welfare policies make it more likely that women and children in poverty will continue to live in poverty.

Seeing Black Feminism

That black women who identify themselves as feminists write plays that represent their views of the world and of important social, political, and cultural issues means that audiences have the opportunity to see black feminist theory on stage, even if they are not conscious of it. Parks, Corthron, and Cleage, who have seen some commercial success, are produced by mainstream regional theatres; these theatres typically stage one play a year by a black playwright.[6] The audiences of these theatres are predominantly white and middle class, and their receptiveness to the issues addressed in the plays varies, as does their ability to understand some of the complexities that these playwrights present. The production of plays like *Flyin' West, Venus,* or *Breath, Boom* in places like Seattle Rep, San Francisco's Curran, London's Royal Court Theatre, or Arena Stage in D.C. means that audiences around the country (and the world) are exposed to black feminist ideas. Cleage and Corthron are also seen by (and accessible to) black audiences, although there are fewer theatres that cater to black audiences around the country.[7]

Some plays are written with particular audiences in mind. Both Holmes and Bridgforth imagine a black audience (usually a black queer audience) for their work; it is more likely to be performed by smaller theatre groups interested in presenting works that feature lesbian, gay, bisexual, or transgender characters. Generally, plays with more overtly same-gender-loving/lesbian-bisexual-gay-trans/queer content are more likely to be produced at small venues. Clarke and Dickerson's play is complex enough that it might be best suited for academic theatres and audiences, where sufficient time can be given to audience education; it is a history lesson, and many might need a road map, but it is most certainly written *for* black women.

Whatever the audience, black feminist theatre does certainly exist. It also has great potential for feminist analysis and critical works rooted in black feminist theories. This project, by examining some exemplars of contemporary black feminist drama and performance, has created a language through which black feminist drama can be recognized and discussed. Perhaps this and other black feminist theories of performance and drama will influence mainstream feminist dramatic theories, opening up the definition of feminist and the scope of what we might call feminist drama and performance.

Notes

Chapter 1: A Black Feminist Theatre Emerges

1. Alain Locke and W. E. B. Du Bois disagreed with the purpose of art, especially for blacks in the United States. While Locke encouraged art for art's sake, regardless of the ways in which blacks were represented (as long as there was truth in them), Du Bois felt that art should always be political and activist, and that drama should aim to engage the struggle against racism and racist representations of blacks.

2. Dana A. Williams's *Contemporary African American Female Playwrights: An Annotated Bibliography*, published in 1998, reveals that the vast majority of black feminist scholarship on black feminist drama has been written by Margaret Wilkerson; to Wilkerson, I would add Glenda Dickerson, Freda Scott Giles, Kathy Perkins, and Judith Stephens as the primary scholars on black feminist drama.

3. Alice Walker's "Definition of Womanism" is very much an influence in generating these elements of this aesthetic. Walker's concept of womanism summarizes the understandings of the intersections of gender, race, class, and sexuality that have informed so many black women writers that preceded Walker, and who have followed her.

Chapter 2: Pearl Cleage's Black Feminism

1. Esther Beth Sullivan has explored the melodramatic elements of *Flyin' West* in her article "The Dimensions of Pearl Cleage's *Flyin' West*." While I understand her argument, I think that the character of Frank is more complicated than a simple villain, which I explain below.

2. Chapter 3 of my *Mammies No More* describes in detail the notion of the "tragic mulatto" in dramas by African American women; this icon is different for men than it is for women.

3. The example that Toni Morrison relates in *Beloved* is not an isolated incident, but rather one example of the desperate measures that some slave women had to use.

4. In 1964, CORE (Congress of Racial Equality), SNCC (Student Nonviolent Coordinating Committee), and the NAACP joined in a project to enfranchise blacks

in Mississippi. During the summer of 1964, more than eighty volunteers, students from northern cities, were beaten; three were murdered by the Ku Klux Klan, and many homes and churches were bombed. As a result of Freedom Summer and those sacrifices, the Voting Rights Act of 1964 was passed.

Chapter 3: We Are the Daughters of Aunt Jemima

1. McDaniel's hope that her Oscar would engender more and better roles for blacks is documented both in Carlton Jackson's *Hattie: The Life of Hattie McDaniel* and in the AMC documentary *Beyond Tara: The Extraordinary Life of Hattie McDaniel.*

2. Indeed, though McDaniel lived a life of relative luxury, other contemporaries who refused such roles, like Butterfly McQueen, actually did work as maids.

3. The reference is to the legend of John Henry, a black slave who worked on the railroad in the mid-nineteenth century; he beat a steam-driving machine, but died after that hard day of work.

4. SCLC, the Southern Christian Leadership Conference, was an organization founded by Martin Luther King Jr.

5. Clarence Thomas was nominated for Supreme Court Justice by Pres. George H. W. Bush. Thomas was nominated because he was conservative and held a "strict constructionist" perspective on the constitution. Thomas had been the head of the Equal Employment Opportunity Commission during the period that had the fewest number of prosecutions for violations of federal equal employment regulations. Hill was an assistant to Thomas during this time; as the only black woman in his office, she was subject to sexual harassment by him while she worked at the EEOC. Hill was not herself a feminist and was very much a conservative. When Thomas was nominated, Hill was convinced by several Democrats and journalists to testify against Thomas and to relate her experience of sexual harassment by him at his nomination hearings. The all-male committee's questions essentially blamed Hill for her own harassment; Thomas declared, in his defense, that he was being "lynched" during the hearings process. He was confirmed in 1991, sparking a cry of protest from black women around the country.

Chapter 4: Battling Images

1. My use of the term "icon" here is semiotic; specifically, it refers to the Peircean concept of an icon as a visual image that "represents its **object** by virtue of a resemblance or similarity" (Colapietro 114). I choose *icon* rather than *index* because iconic signs are related by resemblance, where indexical signs are related by physical or actual connection. Images of black women in U.S. culture resemble actual black women, but are not necessarily related by physical or actual connection.

2. The backward movement of the scene numbers contrasts with the generally forward linear movement of time through the play.

3. This particular aspect of the romanticization of Venus's and the Baron's relationship reminds me of the romanticization of the relationship between Sally Hemmings and Thomas Jefferson, particularly because Venus and the Baron spend this time in Paris, where Jefferson was most free to pursue Hemmings.

4. The Moynihan Report was a report on a federal study interested in finding the causes of inner-city poverty; the conclusion was that woman-headed households, which were partially the result of black women's emasculation of black men, were generating poverty.

5. For discussions of the uses of Brechtian techniques in feminist theatre, see especially Diamond, Case, Dolan, and Phelan.

6. In the original Broadway production, "Old Man River" was sung by Paul Robeson; Robeson's recording has become the classic rendition of the song. He reportedly changed the words of the song, so that "black folks work on the Mississippi" replaced Hammerstein's racist "niggers work on the Mississippi."

7. In my southern-rooted family, New Year's Day dinner consisted of foods to improve one's luck in the New Year, including greens, black-eyed peas, cornbread, and chitterlings.

8. This issue of the attempts by black women to achieve a "white" beauty ideal to escape blackness was also an issue in *Re/Membering Aunt Jemima*.

9. She is not the first to do so; in fact, Zora Neale Hurston's play *The First One* also challenges the biblical text about the creation of blackness out of shame. See Hurston's play, which is published in Kathy Perkins's *Black Women Playwrights Before 1950*.

Chapter 5: Kia Corthron's Everyday Black Women

1. Annual playwriting contest seeking the best new play about contemporary race relations. Typically plays receive a staged reading; *Wake Up, Lou Riser* received a full production.

2. Because *Wake Up, Lou Riser* is not available in published form, I include a summary of the play. I will not do this with the other plays, which are available.

3. See especially *Strange Fruit*, a collection of antilynching plays edited by Kathy Perkins and Judith Stephens; in addition, Stephens has a significant body of critical work on antilynching plays.

4. Medgar Evers was a lawyer and civil rights activist in Mississippi, and he and his wife, Myrtie, set up and ran the Jackson, Mississippi, NAACP field office. Evers was assassinated by white supremacist Byron De La Beckwith in June 1963. Two all-white juries in the 1960s were unable to reach a verdict; De La Beckwith was convicted and sentenced to life in prison in 1994.

Denise McNair, Addie Mae Collins, Carole Robertson, and Cynthia Wesley were four young women who were preparing their Sunday school lessons in the basement of the Sixteenth Street Baptist Church in Birmingham in September 1963 when a bomb placed by segregationists exploded, killing them. While the first of the three men who planted the bomb was tried and convicted in 1977, the last two were tried in 2001 and 2002.

5. Because many lynchings were photographed, with the participants clearly visible, the idea that the perpetrators were anonymous is absurd. Many of these photographs were made into postcards or otherwise distributed. See James Allen, ed., *Without Sanctuary: Lynching Photography in America*.

6. Alan Guttmacher Institute, *Into a New World: Young Woman's Sexual and Reproductive Lives*.

7. According to the Alan Guttmacher Institute, 54 percent of women who have abortions in the United States were using contraception when they became pregnant (http://www.agi-usa.org/pubs/fb_induced_abortion.pdf).

8. *Breath, Boom* was published in the November 2001 issue of *American Theatre,* providing it with a large audience of theatre professionals.

9. The three white men convicted of Byrd's murder are the only white people sentenced to die in Texas for killing a black person. According to a CNN report, "The only white man ever executed in Texas for killing a black person was a farmer who killed another white farmer's favorite slave in the 1850s" (http://cnn.com/US/9902/25/dragging.death.04/).

Chapter 6: Signifying Black Lesbians

1. These three terms are not necessarily interchangeable, but they represent distinct affiliations. The term "lesbian" is used by many, but it is not universal; "queer" is generally though more inclusive, because it is an umbrella term that includes lesbian, bisexual, and transgender. "SGL," or same-gender loving, has been adopted by some black lesbian and gay peoples to more accurately reflect the historical presence of same-gender relations among many African peoples.

2. I use "community" in quotation marks because the notion of a single community based on racial or sexual identity is illusory; no group identity that encompasses people only by race or sexuality can be monolithic or encompass all possible variations of identity. For example, the "black community" is supposed to be primarily Democratic in its voting preferences, but black Republicans certainly do exist.

3. The original text of Molefi Asante's *Afrocentricity* regarded homosexuality as a European invention; Francis Cress Welsing's *The Isis Papers* and Nathan and Julia Hare's *The Endangered Black Family* also condemn homosexuality. Asante publicly changed his perspective on homosexuality in 1998, but the text of *Afrocentricity* has not been revised to reflect this, and it remains a core text in Afrocentric thought.

4. See especially *Boy Wives and Female Husbands,* ed. Steven O. Murray and Will Roscoe; see also *Amazon to Zami: Toward a Global Lesbian Feminism,* ed. Monika Reinfelder, for contemporary writings by same-gender-loving women.

5. See *Gender Trouble, Bodies that Matter,* and article "Performative Acts and Gender Constitution," in *Performing Feminisms,* ed. Sue-Ellen Case.

6. The character of Cleo, played by Queen Latifah, is "loud, overbearing, and sexually aggressive" and is also clearly played as butch (Gomez 174).

7. For explanations of the orisha and their characteristics, see Correal and Neimark.

Chapter 7: A Black Feminist Aesthetic

1. Angela Y. Davis, in her autobiography, recalls the dedication of the black teachers at her dilapidated segregated school in Birmingham, Alabama, who made sure to impart to their students the successes and sacrifices of blacks who had come before them.

2. There was, of course, A'Leila Walker, who was a black patron of the Harlem Renaissance, but she was singular in her ability as a black woman to support the arts.

3. Patricia Hill Collins, in *Black Sexual Politics: African Americans, Gender, and the New Racism,* describes "the new racism" as one in which the expression of racism has shifted to global and transnational economies that maintain social hierarchies in which blacks remain at the bottom and where mass media images continue to claim the end of racism while perpetuating racist images of blacks.

4. Many recent studies have noted higher incidences of asthma in inner-city minority youth, partially as a result of exposure to cockroaches and rodents. As an example, see Claudio et al.

5. See, for example, Margot Young, "Reproductive Technologies and the Law: Norplant and the Bad Mother," discussing the case of an African American woman who was on welfare and had a "large" family required by a court order to be implanted with the long-term birth control device.

6. Cleage has been produced at a wide range of regional theatres, including Seattle Repertory Theatre, Arena Stage, and the Alliance Theatre (Atlanta); Corthron has been produced at Center Stage (Baltimore), Arena Stage Old Vat Room; Parks has been produced on Broadway, Actors Theatre of Louisville, and the Public (NYC).

7. Parks's work, particularly her earlier work, is not something most black audiences would go out of their way to see; her experiments with form and structure do not provide narratives often preferred by black audiences.

Bibliography

Alan Gutmacher Institute. *Into a New World: Young Woman's Sexual and Reproductive Lives.* New York: Alan Guttmacher Institute, 1998.

Alba, Richard. *Ethnic Identity: The Transformation of White America.* New Haven, Conn.: Yale University Press, 1990.

Allen, James, ed. *Without Sanctuary: Lynching Photography in America.* Santa Fe, N.Mex.: Twin Palms Publishers, 2002.

Anderson, Lisa M. *Mammies No More: The Changing Image of Black Women on Stage and Screen.* Lanham, Md.: Rowman and Littlefield, 1997.

Asante, Molefi. *Afrocentricity: The Theory of Social Change.* Trenton, N.J.: Africa World Press, 1988.

Ashcroft, Bill, Gareth Griffiths, and Helen Tiffin. *The Empire Writes Back: Theory and Practice in Postcolonial Literatures.* London: Routledge, 1989.

Augustin, Nathalie A. "Learnfare and Black Motherhood: The Social Construction of Deviancy." In *Critical Race Feminism: A Reader,* ed. Adrien Katherine Wing. New York: New York University Press, 1997.

Austin, Gayle. *Feminist Theories for Dramatic Criticism.* Ann Arbor: University of Michigan Press, 1990.

Bashir, Samiya A. "Pearl Cleage's Idlewild Idylls: An Interview." *Black Issues Book Review* (July/August 2001): 16–20.

Blauner, Robert. *Racial Oppression in America.* New York: Harper and Row, 1972.

Bobo, Jacqueline, ed. *Black Feminist Cultural Criticism.* Malden, Mass.: Blackwell, 2001.

Bogle, Donald. *Toms, Coons, Mulattoes, Mammies, and Bucks: An Interpretive History of Blacks in American Films.* 3d ed. New York: Continuum, 1996.

Bogus, Diane. "The Queen B in Black Literature." In *Lesbian Texts and Contexts,* ed. Jay Glasgow. New York: New York University Press, 1990.

Boykin, Keith. *One More River to Cross: Black and Gay in America.* New York: Anchor, 1995.

Bridgforth, Sharon. *blood pudding.* Unpublished manuscript (courtesy of the author), 1998.

Briggs, Jimmie, and Marcia D. Davis. "The Brutal Truth: Putting Domestic Violence on the Black Agenda." *Emerge* 5, no. 11 (1994): 50.

Brown, Lenora Inez. "The Last Word Is Hope." *American Theatre* 18, no. 9 (2001): 54.

Brown-Guillory, Elizabeth. *Their Place on the Stage: Black Women Playwrights in America.* New York: Greenwood Press, 1988.

Bullard, Robert D., Glenn S. Johnson, and Beverly H. Wright. "Confronting Environmental Injustice: It's the Right Thing to Do." *Race, Gender & Class* 5, no. 1 (October 1997): 63.

Burke, Sally. *American Feminist Playwrights: A Critical History.* New York: Twayne, 1996.

Butler, Judith. "Performative Acts and Gender Constitution: An Essay in Phenomenology and Feminist Theory." In *Performing Feminisms: Feminist Critical Theory and Theatre,* ed. Sue-Ellen Case. Baltimore: Johns Hopkins University Press, 1990.

Case, Sue-Ellen. *Feminism and Theatre.* New York: Routledge, 1988.

———. "Towards a Butch-Femme Aesthetic." In *The Lesbian and Gay Studies Reader,* ed. Abelove, Barale, and Halperin. New York: Routledge, 1993.

Childress, Alice. *Wine in the Wilderness.* In *Black Theatre USA: Plays by African Americans 1847 to Today,* ed. James V. Hatch and Ted Shine. Rev. and exp. ed. New York: The Free Press, 1996.

Christian, Barbara. "But What Do We Think We're Doing Anyway?: The State of Black Feminist Criticism(s) or My Version of a Little Bit of History." In *Changing Our Own Words: Essays in Criticism, Theory, and Writing by Black Women,* ed. Cheryl A. Wall. New Brunswick, N.J.: Rutgers University Press, 1989.

———. "The Highs and the Lows of Black Feminist Criticism." In *Reading Black, Reading Feminist: A Critical Anthology,* ed. Henry Louis Gates. New York: Meridian, 1992.

———. "The Race for Theory." In *Haciendo Caras: Making Face, Making Soul,* ed. Gloria Anzaldúa. San Francisco: Aunt Lute Foundation Books, 1990.

Clarke, Breena, and Glenda Dickerson. *Re/membering Aunt Jemima: A Menstrual Show. Contemporary Plays by Women of Color,* ed. Kathy A. Perkins and Roberta Uno. New York: Routledge, 1996.

———. "Re/membering Aunt Jemima: Rescuing the Secret Voice." *Women and Performance: A Journal of Feminist Theory* 6, no. 1 (1993), 11:77–92.

Clarke, Cheryl. "The Failure to Transform: Homophobia in the Black Community." In *Dangerous Liaisons: Blacks, Gays, and the Struggle for Equality,* ed. Eric Brandt. New York: New Press, 1999.

Cleage, Pearl. *Flyin' West and Other Plays.* New York: TCG, 1999.

———. *Mad at Miles: A Blackwoman's Guide to Truth.* Southfield, Mich.: The Cleage Group, 1999.

Colapietro, Vincent. *Glossary of Semiotics.* New York: Paragon House, 1993.

Collins, Patricia Hill. *Black Sexual Politics: African Americans, Gender, and the New Racism.* New York: Routledge, 2004.

Cooper, Anna Julia. "The Status of Woman in America." In *Words of Fire: An Anthology of African American Feminist Thought,* ed. Beverly Guy-Sheftall. New York: The New Press, 1995.

Correal, Tobe Melora. *Finding Soul on the Path of the Orisa: A West African Spiritual Tradition.* New York: The Crossing Press, 2003.

Corthron, Kia. *Breath, Boom*. New York: Dramatists Play Service, 2002.

———. *Come Down Burning*. In *Colored Contradictions: An Anthology of Contemporary African American Plays,* ed. Harry J. Elam Jr. and Robert Alexander. New York: Plume/Penguin, 1996.

———. *Splash Hatch on the E Going Down*. New York: Dramatists Play Service, 2002.

———. *Wake Up, Lou Riser.* Unpublished manuscript, March 1996.

Claudio, Luz, Jeanette A. Stingone, and James Godbold. "Prevalence of Childhood Asthma in Urban Communities: The Impact of Ethnicity and Income." *Annals of Epidemiology* 16, no. 5 (May 2006): 332–40.

Dahl, Mary Karen. *Political Violence in Drama: Classical Models, Contemporary Variations.* Ann Arbor, Mich.: UMI Research Press, 1987.

Dandridge, Dorothy, and Earl Conrad. *Everything and Nothing: The Dorothy Dandridge Tragedy.* New York: Abelard-Schuman, 1970.

Davis, Angela Y. *Angela Davis: An Autobiography.* New York: Bantam Books, 1975.

de Beauvoir, Simone. *The Second Sex,* tr. and ed. H. M. Parshley. New York: Vintage Books, 1989 [1952].

Deren, Maya. *The Divine Horsemen: Living Gods of Haiti.* New York: Chelsea House Publishers, 1970.

Diamond, Elin. "Refusing the Romanticism of Identity: Narrative Interventions in Churchill, Benmussa, Duras." In *Performing Feminisms: Feminist Critical Theory and Theatre,* ed. Sue-Ellen Case. Baltimore: Johns Hopkins University Press, 1990.

Dobie, Kathy. "The Aggressives." *Vibe* (January 2003): 104–11.

Dorfman, Ariel. *Death and the Maiden.* New York: Penguin Books, 1992.

Dubey, Madhu. *Black Women Novelists and the Nationalist Aesthetic.* Bloomington: Indiana University Press, 1994.

Dunn, Lawrence. "Catch a Falling Star: A Review of *Blues for an Alabama Sky.*" *Hyde Park Citizen* 9, no. 19 (April 9, 1998): 10.

Erhart, Julia. "Picturing *What If:* Julie Dash's Speculative Fiction," *Camera Obscura* 38 (1996): 117–31.

Englebrecht, Penelope J. "Lifting Belly Is a Language: The Postmodern Lesbian Subject." *Feminist-Studies* 16, no. 1 (spring 1990): 85–114

Fanon, Frantz. *The Wretched of the Earth,* tr. Constance Farrington. New York: Grove Press, 1963.

Faires, Robert. "Blood Pudding: Seductive Waters." *Austin Chronicle,* April 1998.

Feder, Abigail. "A Radiant Smile from the Lovely Lady: Overdetermined Femininity in 'Ladies' Figure Skating." *TDR: The Drama Review* 38, no. 1 (1994): 62–78.

Findlay, Heather. "Fishes in a Pond: An Interview with Jewell Gomez." In *Femme: Feminists, Lesbians, and Bad Girls.* New York: Routledge, 1997.

Gabel, Leona C. *From Slavery to the Sorbonne and Beyond: The Life and Writings of Anna J. Cooper.* Northampton, Mass.: Department of History, Smith College, 1982.

Garner, Stanton G. *Bodied Spaces: Phenomenology and Performance in Contemporary Drama.* Ithaca, N.Y.: Cornell University Press, 1994.

Giles, Freda Scott. "In Their Own Words: Pearl Cleage and Glenda Dickerson Define Womanist Theater." *Womanist Theory and Research* 2, no. 1, and 2, no. 2 (1996–97). URL: http://www.uga.edu/-womanist/toc2.1_2.2.htm.

———. "The Motion of Herstory: Three Plays by Pearl Cleage." *African American Review* 13, no. 4 (winter 1997):709–12.

Gilman, Sander. "Black Bodies, White Bodies: Toward an Iconography of Female Sexuality in Late Nineteenth-Century Art, Medicine, and Literature." *Critical Inquiry* 12, no. 1 (autumn 1985): 204–42.

Goldberg, David Theo. *Racist Culture: Philosophy and the Politics of Meaning.* Cambridge, Mass.: Blackwell, 1993.

Goldsby, Jackie. "What It Means to Be Colored Me." *Out/Look,* summer 1990.

Gomez, Jewell. "Black Lesbians: Passing, Stereotypes, and Transformation." In *Dangerous Liaisons: Blacks, Gays, and the Struggle for Equality,* ed. Eric Brandt. New York: The New Press, 1999.

Gordon, Lewis R. *Fanon and the Crisis of European Man: An Essay on Philosophy and the Human Sciences.* New York: Routledge, 1995.

Greene, Alexis. *Women Who Write Plays: Interviews with American Dramatists.* New York: Smith and Kraus, 2001.

Greene, Beverly. "African American Lesbian and Bisexual Women." *Journal of Social Issues* 56, no. 2 (2000): 239–49.

Halberstam, Judith. *Female Masculinity.* Durham, N.C.: Duke University Press, 2000.

Hammonds, Evelyn. "Black (W)holes and the Geometry of Black Female Sexuality." *Differences: A Journal of Feminist Cultural Studies* 6, no. 2, 3 (1994): 126–45.

Hansberry, Lorraine. "Simone de Beauvoir and *The Second Sex:* An American Commentary (An Unfinished Essay-in-Progress)." In *Words of Fire: An Anthology of African American Feminist Thought,* ed. Beverly Guy-Sheftall. New York: The New Press, 1995.

Hare, Nathan and Julia. *The Endangered Black Family.* San Francisco: Black Think Tank, 1984.

Harris, Laura, and Elizabeth Crocker, eds. *Femme: Feminists, Lesbians, and Bad Girls.* New York: Routledge, 1997.

Hill, Errol, and James Hatch. *A History of African American Theatre.* New York: Cambridge, 2003.

Holmes, Shirlene. *A Lady and a Woman.* In *Amazon All Stars: Thirteen Lesbian Plays,* ed. Rosemary Keefe Curb. New York: Applause, 1996.

hooks, bell. "Postmodern Blackness." In *Yearning: Race, Gender, and Cultural Politics.* Boston: South End Press, 1990.

Inness, Sherrie A. *The Lesbian Menace: Ideology, Identity and the Representation of Lesbian Life.* Amherst: University of Massachusetts Press, 1997.

Jackson, Carlton. *Hattie: The Life of Hattie McDaniel.* Lanham, Md.: Madison Books, 1990.

Jeffries, Susan. *Not a Passing Phase: Reclaiming Lesbians in History 1840–1985.* New York: Trafalgar Square Books, 1989.

Jewell, K. Sue. *From Mammy to Miss America and Beyond: Cultural Images and the Shaping of U.S. Social Policy.* New York: Routledge, 1993.

Johnson, Maria V. "Pouring Out the Blues: Gwen 'Sugar Mama' Avery's Song of Freedom." *Frontiers: A Journal of Women's Studies* 25, no. 1 (2004): 93–110.

Jones, Beth A., et al. "African American/White Differences in Breast Carcinoma: Alterations and Other Tumor Characteristics." *CANCER.* Published online 9 August 2004 (DOI: 10.1002/cncr.20500). Print issue date 15 September 2004.

Lahr, John. Review of *Venus, A Play,* by Suzan-Lori Parks. *New Yorker* 72 (20 May 1996): 98.

Langworthy, Douglas. "Making Our History: An Interview with the Playwright." *American Theatre* 13, no. 6 (July/August 1996): 21–23.

Lester, Neal. "Shange's Men: *for colored girls* Revisited, and Movement Beyond." *African American Review* 26, no. 2 (1992): 319–28.

Lorde, Audre. *Sister Outsider.* Trumansburg, N.Y.: Crossing Press, 1984.

Marsh-Lockett, Carol P. *Black Women Playwrights: Visions on the American Stage.* New York: Garland, 1999.

Maseko, Zola (director/writer). *The Life and Times of Sara Baartman.* First Run/Icarus Films: West Glen Films, 1998, videocassette.

Mays, Vickie M., Susan D. Cochran, and Sylvia Rhue. "Impact of Perceived Discrimination on the Intimate Relationships of Black Lesbians." *Journal of Homosexuality* 25, no. 4 (1993): 1–14.

McCroy, Winnie. "Exploring a Bulldagger's Experience." *Baltimore Gay Paper,* August 1998.

Miller, William Lee. *Arguing about Slavery: The Great Battle in the United States Congress.* New York: Alfred A. Knopf, 1996.

Milos, Marilyn Fayre, ed. *Nocirc Newsletter,* 6.1 (Spring 1992). www.nocirc.org/publish/3-92.pdf

Minh-ha, Trinh, T. "The Other Censorship." In *When the Moon Waxes Red.* New York: Routledge, 1991.

Morgan, Joan. *When Chickenheads Come Home to Roost: My Life as a Hip-Hop Feminist.* New York: Simon and Schuster, 1999.

Morrison, Toni. *Playing in the Dark: Whiteness and the Literary Imagination.* Cambridge, Mass.: Harvard University Press, 1992.

Moss, Barbara P. "How the African American Storyteller Impacts the Black Family and Society." Yale–New Haven Teachers Institute. http://www.yale.edu/ynhti/curriculum/units/1990/4/90.04.05.x.html. Accessed 5 January 2004.

Murray, Steven O., and Will Roscoe. *Boy Wives and Female Husbands.* New York: Palgrave Macmillan, 1998.

National Institutes of Health. "Large Portion of Late-Stage Breast Cancers Associated With Absence of Screening." http://www.nih.gov/news/pr/oct2004/nci-19.htm. Accessed 13 June 2005.

National Cancer Institute. "A Snapshot of Cervical Cancer." http://prg.nci.nih.gov/snapshots/Cervical-Snapshot.pdf. Accessed 13 June 2005.

Neimark, Philip John. *The Way of the Orisa: Empowering Your Life through the Ancient African Religion of Ifa.* San Francisco: HarperSanFrancisco, 1993.

Parks, Sheri. "In My Mother's House: Black Feminist Aesthetics, Television, and *A Raisin in the Sun.*" In *Theatre and Feminist Aesthetics,* ed. Karen Laughlin and Catherine Schuler. Madison and Teaneck, N.J.: Farleigh Dickinson University Press, 1995.

Parks, Suzan-Lori. *The Death of the Last Black Man in the Whole Entire World.* In *The America Play and Other Plays.* New York: TCG Press, 1995.

———. *In the Blood.* In *The Red Letter Plays.* New York: TCG Press, 2001.

———. *Venus: A Play.* New York: TCG Press, 1997.

Perkins, Kathy. *Black Women Playwrights before 1950*. Bloomington: Indiana University Press, 1991.

Perkins, Kathy, and Judith Stephens, eds. *Strange Fruit*. Bloomington: Indiana University Press, 1998.

Phelan, Peggy. *Unmarked: The Politics of Performance*. New York: Routledge, 1993.

Pieterse, Jan Nederveen. *White on Black: Images of Africans and Blacks in Western Popular Culture*. New Haven, Conn.: Yale University Press, 1993.

Porter, Adina. Interview. 14 May 1996.

Quinion, Michael. "Dysmorphia." In *World Wide Words,* http://www.quinion.com/words/turnsofphrase/tp-mus1.htm. Accessed 21 October 2003.

Reinfelder, Monika. *Amazon to Zami: Toward a Global Lesbian Feminism*. London: Cassell, 1996.

Rhodes, Jewell Parker. *Voodoo Dreams: A Novel of Marie Laveau*. New York: St. Martin's Press, 1993.

Richardson, Mattie Udora. "No More Secrets, No More Lies: African American History and Compulsory Heterosexuality." *Journal of Women's History* 15, no. 3 (autumn 2003): 63–76.

Roberts, Dorothy E. "The Future of Reproductive Choice for Poor Women and Women of Color." In *The Politics of Women's Bodies: Sexuality, Appearance, and Behavior,* ed. Rose Weitz. 2d ed. New York: Oxford University Press, 2003.

Ross, Loretta J. "African American Women and Abortion: 1800–1970." In *Theorizing Black Feminisms: The Visionary Pragmatism of Black Women,* ed. Stanlie M. James and Abena P. A. Busia. London: Routledge, 1993.

Sanders, Pamela D. "Beyond Representations of the Black Bourgeoisie: Race, Color, Gender, and Class in the Works of Dorothy West." Master's thesis, Purdue University, 1998.

Sawyer, Ethel. "A Study of a Public Lesbian Community." Master's thesis, Washington University, 1965.

Setshwaelo, Marang. "The Return of the Hottentot Venus." Africana.com. www.africana.com/DailyArticles/index_20020214.htm. Accessed 14 February 2002.

Shakur, Assatta. *Assata: An Autobiography*. Westport, Conn.: L. Hill, 1987.

Shange, Ntozake. *for colored girls who have considered suicide/when the rainbow is enuf.* New York: Collier Books, 1989 [1977].

Shinn, Thelma J. "Living the Answer: The Emergence of African American Feminist Drama." *Studies in the Humanities* 17 (December 1990): 149–59.

Siegel, Ed. "Ambitious 'Blood' Enriches An Old Tale." *Boston Globe,* March 28, 2002, D3.

Smith, Barbara. *The Truth That Never Hurts: Writings on Race, Gender, and Freedom*. New Brunswick, N.J.: Rutgers University Press, 1998.

Smothers, Ronald. "Teenage Girl Fatally Stabbed at a Bus Stop in Newark." *New York Times,* Tuesday, May 13, 2003, Section B, 8.

Spencer, Suzy. "Other Voices, Other Rooms." *Austin Chronicle,* July 28, 2000, 52–54.

Strother, Z. S. "Display of the Body Hottentot." In *Africans on Stage: Studies in Ethnological Show Business*. Bloomington: Indiana University Press, 1999.

Sullivan, Esther Beth. "The Dimensions of Pearl Cleage's *Flyin' West*." *Theatre Topics* 7, no. 1 (1997): 11–22.

Swarns, Rachel L. "Census Portrait of Gay Couples Who Are Black." *New York Times,* Thursday, October 27, 2004, Section A, 24.

Takaki, Ronald. *A Different Mirror: A History of Multicultural America.* New York: Little, Brown, 1992.

Terrell, Mary Church. "The Progress of Colored Women." In *Words of Fire: An Anthology of African American Feminist Thought,* ed. Beverly Guy-Sheftall. New York: The New Press, 1995.

Venkatesh, Sudhir Alladi. "Gender and Outlaw Capitalism: A Historical Account of the Black Sisters United Girl Gang." *Signs: Journal of Women in Culture and Society* 23, no. 3 (1988): 683–709.

Walker, Alice. "Definition of Womanist." In *Making Face, Making Soul/Haciendo Caras: Creative and Critical Perspectives by Feminists of Color,* ed. Gloria Anzaldúa. San Francisco: Aunt Lute Books, 1990.

Wallace, Michelle. "The Hottentot Venus." *Village Voice,* May 21, 1996, 31.

———. "Variations on Negation and the Heresy of Black Feminist Creativity." In *Reading Black, Reading Feminist: A Critical Anthology,* ed. Henry Louis Gates. New York: Meridian, 1990.

Wattleton, Faye. *Life on the Line.* New York: Random House, 1996.

Welsing, Francis Cress. *The Isis Papers.* Chicago: Third World Press, 1991.

Wilkerson, Margaret B. "Introduction." In *Lorraine Hansberry: The Collected Last Plays,* ed. Robert Nemiroff. New York: Plume, 1983.

Williams, Dana A. *Contemporary African American Female Playwrights: An Annotated Bibliography.* Westport, Conn.: Greenwood Press, 1998.

Williams, Richard E. *Called and Chosen: The Story of Mother Rebecca Jackson and the Philadelphia Shakers.* Metuchen, N.J.: Scarecrow Press, 1981.

Williams, Sherley Anne. "Some Implications of Womanist Theory." In *Reading Black, Reading Feminist: A Critical Anthology,* ed. Henry Louis Gates. New York: Meridian, 1990.

Wing, Adrien Katherine, ed. *Critical Race Feminism: A Reader.* New York: New York University Press, 1997.

Wing, Adrien Katherine, and Christine A. Willis. "Sisters in the Hood: Beyond Bloods and Crips." In *Critical Race Feminism: A Reader.* New York: New York University Press, 1997.

Young, Jean. "The Re-Objectification and Re-Commodification of Saartjie Baartman in Suzan-Lori Parks's *Venus.*" *African American Review* 31, no. 4 (winter 1997): 699–708.

Young, Margot. "Reproductive Technologies and the Law: Norplant and the Bad Mother." *Marriage and Family Review* 21, no. 3 (1995): 259–81.

Index

"aggressives," 98, 105
American immigrant dream, 71
anti-lynching plays, 6, 79–80

Baartman, Sara, 57–59, 60, 118
Baker, Ella, 51
beauty, 38–39, 73
black aesthetic, 2, 11
black feminist aesthetic, 2–4, 12–16,
  31–32, 71, 111, 115–16
black feminist literary criticism, 12
black women in popular culture, 13,
  35–42, 51–53, 63, 110, 119
black women's health, 44–48, 121
Bluest Eye, The (Morrison), 43
"bo akutia," 36
Bobo, Jacqueline, 12
Brechtian techniques, 72–72
Bullins, Ed, 97, 110; *Clara's Ole Man,* 97
Bumpers, Eleanor, 46
"butch" embodiment, 105
Butler, Judith, 104

Childress, Alice, 3, 9–10, 11, 120
Christian, Barbara, 1, 3, 12, 14, 17
civil rights era, 7; black feminist plays
  in, 7–9
Clarke, Cheryl, 97
Collins, Patricia Hill, 1, 100, 106, 117–18;
  and "the new racism," 117, 131n3
Cooper, Anna Julia, 4, 48–50, 53, 118
critical race feminism, 15, 46, 76–77

Dandridge, Dorothy, 41–42, 119
Davis, Angela, 50–51
domestic violence, 18–23, 88–89, 121–22
Dubey, Madhu, 3, 11
Du Bois–Locke debate, 2

Ellis, Ruth, 95
environmental racism, 84–85, 121
Exodus of 1879, 18–19

female circumcision, 45–46
feminist dramatic criticism, 13, 104–5, 126
"femme" identity, 109–11; and "passing,"
  110

Giles, Freda Scott, 14, 25
Gomez, Jewell, 97, 104
Gone With the Wind (1939 film), 39
Gunn, Sakia, 98

Hamer, Fannie Lou, 51
Hansberry, Lorraine, 3, 7–9
Harlem renaissance, 5–6, 25–29; black
  feminist plays in, 6
Harris, Trudier, 31
Hill, Anita, 52, 128n5
homophobia, 28–29, 97–99
hooks, bell, 2

Imitation of Life (1934 film), 38, 43
Inness, Sherrie, 105
intersectionality, 4, 8, 14, 18–21, 71

Jackson, Mother Rebecca, 49, 118

Kennedy, Adrienne, 9, 13, 75
Ku Klux Klan, 77–81

lesbian and gay history, 28, 34, 113–14
lesbian gender (butch/femme), 99, 104–11
Lester, Neal, 10
Leveau, Marie, 42–43
Lorde, Audre, 13, 110
lynching, 5–6, 72, 79–80

"mammy," 38–40, 52, 119
McDaniel, Hattie, 39–40
melodrama, use of, 19, 23–24, 41
Morgan, Joan, 14
Mulatto (Hughes), 20, 24
myth of the black matriarchy, 9, 51

nineteenth-century black feminism, 4

Perkins, Kathy, 5
post-traumatic stress disorder and black
    men, 11, 33
poverty, 24, 90, 119–21, 125. *See also*
    TANF; "welfare queen"

rape, 6, 10, 18, 41, 92
reproductive rights, 6, 8, 25–28, 31, 44–45,
    63–64, 85–87, 122–23; teen pregnancy
    and, 81–83, 124–25
Rhodes, Jewell Parker, 42

Sawyer, Ethel, 104
Set It Off (1996 film), 105, 110
sexuality, 10–11, 25, 31–32, 40, 42, 44–45,
    55–59, 63–64, 96–97, 103, 104, 123–24
sexual violence/abuse, 43, 57, 59–61, 65,
    87–88, 92, 102
Shange, Ntozake, 1, 9, 10–11
Simone, Nina, 47
Smith, Barbara, 2, 12, 95
Stephens, Judith, 5

TANF (Temporary Aid to Needy Fami-
    lies), 65, 82, 121
Terrell, Mary Church, 4
"tragic" mulatto/a, 19–23, 36, 41–44, 119
Tubman, Harriet, 49

violence, 67–70, 117–18; and girl gangs,
    87–90, 92, 125; racist, 32–33, 34, 79–81,
    91, 125; staged, 91–94

Wattleton, Faye, 44–45
Welbon, Yvonne, 95, 114
"welfare queen," 55, 65–70
West, Cheryl, 96
Wilkerson, Margaret, 8, 127n2
Wine in the Wilderness (Childress), 9–10,
    120
womanism, 8, 13

LISA M. ANDERSON is an associate professor in women's studies and theater at Arizona State University. She is the author of *Mammies No More: The Changing Image of Black Women on Stage and Screen*.

The University of Illinois Press
is a founding member of the
Association of American University Presses.

———————————————

Composed in 10.3/13 Hoefler Text
with Myriad Pro display
by Jim Proefrock
at the University of Illinois Press
Manufactured by Thomson-Shore, Inc.

University of Illinois Press
1325 South Oak Street
Champaign, IL 61820-6903
www.press.uillinois.edu